T0311766

Cambridge Elements ⹀

Elements in the Renaissance
edited by
John Henderson
Birkbeck, University of London, and Wolfson College, University of Cambridge
Jonathan K. Nelson
Syracuse University Florence, and Kennedy School, Harvard University

THE RENAISSANCE ON THE ROAD

Mobility, Migration and Cultural Exchange

Rosa Salzberg
University of Trento

CAMBRIDGE
UNIVERSITY PRESS

Shaftesbury Road, Cambridge CB2 8EA, United Kingdom

One Liberty Plaza, 20th Floor, New York, NY 10006, USA

477 Williamstown Road, Port Melbourne, VIC 3207, Australia

314–321, 3rd Floor, Plot 3, Splendor Forum, Jasola District Centre, New Delhi – 110025, India

103 Penang Road, #05–06/07, Visioncrest Commercial, Singapore 238467

Cambridge University Press is part of Cambridge University Press & Assessment, a department of the University of Cambridge.

We share the University's mission to contribute to society through the pursuit of education, learning and research at the highest international levels of excellence.

www.cambridge.org
Information on this title: www.cambridge.org/9781108965668

DOI: 10.1017/9781108963886

First published 2023

A catalogue record for this publication is available from the British Library.

ISBN 978-1-108-96566-8 Paperback
ISSN 2631-9101 (online)
ISSN 2631-9098 (print)

The Renaissance on the Road

Mobility, Migration and Cultural Exchange

Elements in the Renaissance

DOI: 10.1017/9781108963886
First published online: June 2023

Rosa Salzberg
University of Trento

Author for correspondence: Rosa Salzberg, rosa.salzberg@unitn.it

Abstract: The Renaissance was a highly mobile, turbulent era in Europe, when war, poverty, and persecution pushed many people onto the roads in search of a living or a safe place to settle. In the same period, the expansion of European states overseas opened up new avenues of long-distance migration while also fuelling the global traffic in slaves. The accelerating movement of people stimulated commercial, political, religious, and artistic exchanges while also prompting the establishment of new structures of control and surveillance. This Element illuminates the material and social mechanisms that enacted mobility in the Renaissance and thereby offers a new way to understand the period's dynamism, creativity, and conflict. Spurred by recent 'mobilities' studies, it highlights the experiences of a wide range of mobile populations, paying particular attention to the concrete, practical dimensions of moving around at this time, whether on a local or a global scale.

Keywords: migration, mobility, Europe, Renaissance, cultural exchange

ISBNs: 9781108965668 (PB), 9781108963886 (OC)
ISSNs: 2631-9101 (online), 2631-9098 (print)

Contents

Introduction

In many ways, the early Commedia dell'arte character of the Zanni, as he emerged in the second half of the sixteenth century, represents an archetypal Renaissance migrant. In the scenarios of the Commedia and the cheap pamphlets and street performances that also recounted his exploits, Zanni is usually depicted as a poor man forced to leave the rural penury and chronic hunger of his home in the mountains of the Bergamasco region and head towards a rich city of the northern Italian plain, often Venice. Travelling on foot, he encounters all the travails of the road, from bad weather to bandits. In one pamphlet, he takes refuge at a rural inn, where he enters into conversation with other travellers from Mantua, Ferrara, Greece, Venice, and elsewhere; a comedic cacophony of different accents and dialects ensues (*Disgrazie del Zane*, undated). In another, Zanni reaches the city and is dazzled by its noise, crowds, and abundance of goods (*Viaggio de Zan Padella*, [1580]). In the sophisticated metropolis, his rustic dialect marks him out immediately as a poor migrant from the rural periphery. Nonetheless, in other scenarios Zanni finds work as a porter (*facchino*) or as the servant of a rich merchant such as the Pantalone character. This employment sometimes takes him on additional journeys, perhaps across the Mediterranean on a trading voyage, serving for a time as a soldier in a travelling army, working as a sailor, or even ending up a captive slave.[1]

Zanni's migrations made him a vector of relations between the rural and urban worlds, an interlocuter in numerous multilingual, multicultural, and cross-class exchanges, as well as a flexible provider of the kinds of menial labour that were essential to the functioning of Renaissance cities and states. In this way, Zanni reflects – in comic mode – the experiences of a great many people in this period, whose moves, whether temporary or permanent, had significant consequences both for their own lives and in shaping the world around them. Moreover, Zanni also exemplifies a particular kind of cultural mobility; as Commedia actors travelled across the continent, turning this performance tradition into a pan-European phenomenon, the Zanni character also followed its own trajectories, spawning the celebrated figure of Arlecchino/Harlequin (see Figure 1).[2]

As Zanni's peregrinations remind us, too, the period circa 1450–1650 that we call the Renaissance was a highly mobile, turbulent era in Europe, when war, famine, land enclosures, and religious persecution pushed many onto the roads

---

[1] On Zanni's travels, see Henke (2015: 75–7); Jaffe-Berg (2016); Salzberg (2017); and for various texts and scenarios, see Pandolfi (1957).

[2] Henke (1991). On this image, of a destitute Arlecchino on the road with his children strapped into a basket on his back, see Henke (2015: 119).

Figure 1 Arlecchino on the road. From Tristano Martinelli, *Compositions de rhetorique*, Lyon, 1601, 48. By permission of the Bibliothèque Nationale de France.

in search of a living or a safe place to settle. For numerous people, as for the Zanni, 'stability was a privilege' (Page Moch, 1992: 2), while being 'unsettled' was an increasingly common experience (Fumerton, 2006). Even if Medieval Europe was already 'a world of unceasing movement' (Verdon, 1998: 6), factors such as commercialization, state formation, and globalization spurred a significant increase in the frequency, scale, and speed of mobility from the later fifteenth century and throughout the Renaissance and Early Modern period (Lucassen & Lucassen, 2009).[3] From the sixteenth century in particular we can observe the further development of transport and hospitality infrastructures across the continent, helping to accelerate the movement of people and goods.

---

[3] On Medieval mobility, see also Moatti (2004); Preiser-Kapeller, Reinfandt and Stouraitis (2020).

While pilgrimage remained a popular practice throughout this period for both women and men, new forms of travel for pleasure, curiosity, or education also became more and more common (Maczak, 1995; Roche, 2003). At the same time, the expansion of European states overseas opened up new avenues for settlers, soldiers, merchants, bureaucrats, and missionaries to move across the globe, as 'oceans became bridges rather than barriers to continents' (Parker, 2010: 86), while also fuelling the global traffic in slaves. Meanwhile, in Europe itself, new systems and technologies, from the postal service to the printing press, sped up the transmission of information, changing perceptions of distance and time (Behringer, 2006; Scott, 2015).

The ever-greater movement of people and goods stimulated the kinds of commercial, political, religious, and artistic encounters and exchanges that we have come to associate with the Renaissance period. Increasingly fast and multi-directional movement fostered prosperity, growth, and innovation. At the same time, however, accelerating mobility prompted the establishment of new structures of control and surveillance, expressing the 'desire to establish boundaries, to demarcate and dominate' (Martin & Bleichmar, 2016: 618). Mobility connected and enabled but it also disrupted and threatened established systems, identities, and beliefs (Young Kim, 2014: 7). States, regions, and cities worked hard to make the most of the opportunities afforded by allowing people and commodities to move to and through them, but they simultaneously strove to limit, block, or at least monitor some of these flows. They established mechanisms – some still in use today – to contain the spread of diseases, the diffusion of 'dangerous' ideas, and the arrival of unwanted migrants who might strain local resources. The mobile poor, along with other itinerant groups such as gypsies, were increasingly criminalized and persecuted (Hitchcock, 2020). The intersection and creative tension between these various crosscurrents fundamentally shaped the lives, itineraries, and experiences of mobile individuals in this period. They also left lasting traces on many other aspects of Renaissance life: on settled communities, on urban and rural landscapes, and on cultural formations.

Unravelling this continuous tension between mobility and efforts to stop or slow movement offers a new way to think about and understand the dynamism, creativity, and conflict of the Renaissance period. In this, we can take inspiration from recent research in the social sciences and humanities which provides fresh models for approaching the study of mobility, under the rubric of the 'mobilities paradigm'.[4] This body of work insists on an understanding of movement as an integral part of human societies: as the norm rather than the exception. It draws

---

[4] For useful overviews, see Urry (2007); Adey et al. (2014).

our attention to practices of mobility and to their impact on people, politics, culture, and the environment. It also encourages conversations between disparate branches of scholarship – on transport, communication, travel, or migration, for example (Pooley, 2017). It thereby makes more apparent the intersecting systems and structures of mobility that underpinned even the most apparently disconnected places and settled lives.

Certain kinds of mobility have been central to the study of this period at least since the 1990s. Around this time, scholars began to emphasize a vision of the Renaissance as 'a remarkably international, fluid, and mobile phenomenon' (Brotton, 2002: 19) as a result of escalating transfers of people, styles, techniques, texts, and especially luxury goods between Europe and the wider world.[5] More recent research has probed the significance of Renaissance mobility in new ways, drawing on spatial, material, and sensorial approaches to help us understand what it meant to move at this time and what impact that movement had, as well as shedding light on the experiences of more ordinary migrants and those who were forced to move against their will because of poverty, persecution, or slavery. Recent overviews of Renaissance culture have given more space to the mobility of ideas and objects (manuscripts and antiquities, for example) as well as paying attention to how physical mobility promoted interactions between centres and peripheries and between learned and uneducated social spheres (e.g. Ruggiero, 2015; Cox, 2016). Various projects and publications have examined in detail the translation and 'migration' of texts across Europe as well as the movement of art objects and manufactured goods that underpinned the spread of Renaissance culture (Helmstutler Di Dio, 2015; Martin & Bleichmar, 2016; Fraser, 2020). Important work has highlighted the cultural influence of highly mobile groups such as artists (Young Kim, 2014), religious refugees (Terpstra, 2015), itinerant performers (Degl'Innocenti & Rospocher, 2019a), and exiled intellectuals (Burke, 2017), as well as the social, political, and economic impact of immigration to Europe's growing cities, especially of artisans and other workers (Luu, 2005; De Munck & Winter, 2012). The long-flourishing field of research on travel writing has begun to expand to examine a wider range of travellers and texts (Holmberg, 2019; Gelléri & Willie, 2021).

Still under-examined are what we might call the 'quotidian mechanics' of moving around at this time: the material and physical experiences as well as the structures, technologies, and practices that facilitated, or impeded, mobility, whether on a local or a global scale (Nelles & Salzberg, 2023). As Stephen Greenblatt stressed, before examining the cultural transfers that it engenders,

---

[5] For an overview of this scholarship, see Trivellato (2010).

mobility needs first to be studied in a highly literal sense and these practical aspects seen as 'indispensable keys to understanding the fate of cultures' (2010: 250). In other words, to better understand the impact of mobility and what it meant to people at the time, we need to know more about what it felt like and how it *worked* (or did not), in a very concrete sense.

Applying a 'mobilities lens' to the Renaissance implies a move away from a more fixed perspective focused on the achievements of major capitals or leading individuals. Instead, it suggests that we follow some of the wanderers on their travels, while also casting an eye back to how the centre looks from a more peripheral, more mobile point of view. It means resting our gaze on liminal, in-between moments in people's lives (examining journeys, not just destinations) and slowing down transfers to examine their constituent parts. This approach shows how even what previously seemed fixed and solid was more contingent and malleable than we might once have thought, shaped by the continuous movement that flowed around, under, or through it.

Closer examination of practices and experiences of mobility reminds us that 'while movement was common' in this period, 'it often proved difficult, dangerous, laborious, and slow – aspects that can be easily overlooked in our instantaneous digital age' (Martin & Bleichmar, 2016: 608). Even as it became easier and faster to move across long distances in the Renaissance, that movement was never smooth or 'frictionless'. Rather, it was interrupted by numerous obstacles and delays: from the mundane (waiting for documents to be checked or for a ship to depart) to the dramatic (a violent storm, an outbreak of plague, or an armed conflict). Travel, even by the fastest methods available, took time, and weather or other adversities could make it take even longer. And yet, this friction could also be a creative force, provoking encounters and confrontations.

As our own times make plain, we need to be careful not to promote a triumphalist narrative about increasing mobility and global interconnectedness. Looking beyond the border crossers and go-betweens, we also must seek to understand the intertwined phenomenon of rootedness and how accelerating mobility spurred the assertion of identities and differences (Greenblatt, 2010: 252; Ghobrial, 2019). Attentive to this, studying mobility can in fact help us to better understand local identities and communities which were often defined in relation to extraneous or mobile 'others'. As recent scholarship has stressed, even those who seemingly 'stayed put' in their native place might still be highly mobile on a small scale (Faroqhi, 2014), while some of the most active cross-cultural brokers led relatively sedentary lives (Raj, 2016). We can see this inextricable interweaving of mobility and immobility evidenced also in Renaissance cities, whose solid forms were moulded by the 'micro-mobilities' of people and things – movements which can be examined to reveal dynamics of power, gender difference, belonging, or exclusion (De Vivo, 2016; Gonzalez Martin, Salzberg & Zenobi, 2021; Nevola, 2021). Even rural areas which were seemingly more static and socially homogeneous than the era's multi-ethnic urban centres could be indelibly marked by the passage of people, carts, or boats, their societies and cultures shaped by their role as border lands or transit zones (Scholz, 2020).

This Element seeks to illuminate the material and social mechanisms that enacted mobility in the Renaissance. Spurred by recent 'mobilities' studies, it looks at different kinds of mobility and of mobile people alongside each other. This is done with the conviction that the treatment and experiences of various mobile groups were interconnected and intertwined – that motives for moving can be hard to discern or disentangle. For instance, peasants travelling in and out of cities to sell their produce at the market also carried news and gossip between rural and urban worlds (Hewlett, 2016); European merchants operating in the East also went on pilgrimage to the holy sites of Christianity, while pilgrims both Christian and Muslim often engaged in some trading or shopping on the side (Bianchi & Howard, 2003; Faroqhi, 2014); humanist scholars travelled not just to teach or study, to visit libraries or cultural sites, but also to contract with printers for the publication of their works and to escape war, persecution, or plague (Stagl, 2002; Burke, 2017).

While it can be hard to separate distinct types of mobility or migration, it is nonetheless vital to emphasize that experiences of moving differed greatly depending on factors such as age, sex, race, class, and religion.[6] Likely even more meaningful were the distinctions between those who chose to move, those who fled (refugees, persecuted religious minorities), and those who were forcibly moved or removed (vagrants, slaves, Indigenous peoples). Moving, of course, is a radically different experience depending on whether one intends to or can return home or not; goes alone or with familiar companions; is welcomed or shunned in new places; and has the means to move comfortably or not. And still, many travellers might share important things in common: for example, interacting with the same regimes of identification, mixing in the same spaces of hospitality or transport, or needing to negotiate linguistic and cultural boundaries. It is thus helpful to consider some of these common structures and challenges, even while remaining aware of the critical differences with which people faced or overcame them.

This Element aims to give a sense of the many reasons for moving in this period and the role that mobility played in the daily lives of many people. It also

---

[6] For an important recent discussion of connections between race and mobility in this period, see Das et al. (2021).

hopes to offer new insight into the social and cultural life of the era, by illuminating some of the mechanisms that facilitated and shaped the trajectories of renowned figures as well as 'ordinary' people and brought them into contact with each other. Even as it concentrates on people in motion – and, to a lesser extent, on the movement of things – by doing so it hopes to unpack some of the 'invisible baggage' that travelled along with them: ideas, styles, knowledge, skills. While the principal zone of interest is continental Europe and Britain, the Element also casts an eye towards the escalating connections with the wider world, with the hope of understanding how European mobility in this period fitted into broader, global currents.

But how can we follow mobile people, who slip across borders and jurisdictions? Archival sources tend to be written from the settled point of view of those in power, and thus much scholarship has naturally adopted this perspective. However, documents can also be read to illuminate the people coming and going out of a particular territory, especially as increasing efforts to control mobility in this period left more and more documentary traces of them (Rollison, 1999). Travel diaries and guidebooks have been used to explore the experiences and mentalities of pilgrims and proto-tourists, even as these necessarily represent a privileged upper stratum of Renaissance society: people generally literate and wealthy enough to travel out of choice rather than necessity. But such sources can also be mined for information about others who accompanied or served the diary writers and guidebook users or who shared space with them in inns, boats, or on the road (Verhoeven, 2019). While it is extremely difficult to access the subjective experience of most individuals who moved in this period (highly mobile groups such as domestic servants, artisans, sailors, soldiers, labourers, and many other, often illiterate, migrants), we can shed some light on their movements through a variety of sources, from images to architecture to literature. And again, while evidence privileges the experiences of those who chose to move, recent work shows that it is possible to know something of the numerous involuntary migrants of this period, such as slaves, deportees, and refugees (McKee, 2008; Terpstra, 2015; Hitchcock, 2016; Barker, 2019). Mobile people also sometimes left traces on the rural and urban landscapes through which they passed, which can provide evidence of their itineraries and experiences: from the family crests of nobles affixed to the interiors of inns in which they stayed (Meer, 2021) to the graffiti of merchants and sailors on the walls of lazzaretti where they were forced to spend time in quarantine (Malagnini, 2017).

The Element is divided into three sections. The first, 'Infrastructures', explores the physical sites and social processes that enabled, obstructed, or channelled the movement of people in the Renaissance. Exploring spaces of transport (roads and water systems) and hospitality (inns, hostels, lodging houses), as well as sites of control (gates, customs points, quarantine stations), it suggests how the development of mobility infrastructure in the period shaped both urban and rural landscapes and provided focal points of interaction between people on the move and more settled communities. As contemporary mobilities scholars have argued, such infrastructures worked to '"channel" and select, offering privileged access for some and barriers for others, leading to a multiplication of borders and creating differential inclusion' (Meeus, Van Heur & Arnaut, 2019: 23). At the same time, in the Renaissance even more so than today, these infrastructures were not all planned, imposed, and regulated from above by powerful state, city, or regional authorities. In many cases, they were created and maintained by small communities and individual operators and were actively engaged with by migrants and travellers themselves.

The second section, 'Materialities', considers the physical, sensorial experience of moving bodies across distances, as well as the things that people carried with or on them, from clothes and luggage to guidebooks and travel documents. It argues that although there was a great range of levels of comfort or hardship and many kinds of reception offered to people on the move in the Renaissance (spanning from warm welcome to hostile rejection), there were similarly some common elements in the experience of mobility. It also considers how even temporary changes to one's external appearance, habits, and customs while travelling could leave more enduring marks on a person's body and identity.

The final section, 'Agents of Exchange', explores the work of some vital – but often neglected – brokers of mobility and cultural exchange, such as pedlars, itinerant performers, interpreters, innkeepers, and postmasters. These range from highly mobile to more sedentary figures who nonetheless operated as crucial mediators, supporting the movements of others as well as brokering interactions between people on the move and settled communities. While their personal experiences of migration and mobility allowed many of these individuals to act as effective enablers of a great array of cultural, economic, and social exchanges, it could also make them subject to suspicion and resentment. This in turn underlines the ambivalence and tension surrounding physical mobility in the Renaissance, as a practice that could lead to immensely profitable and creative outcomes but also engender new challenges and conflicts.

1 Infrastructures

Like many Renaissance artists, mobility was essential to the life and career of the Florentine goldsmith and sculptor Benvenuto Cellini (1500–71). Although more famous for its dramatic episodes of violence and sex, Cellini's celebrated autobiography also relates his numerous peregrinations around the Italian states and as far as France: to train, to work, to flee the law or his enemies, and sometimes just for pleasure or curiosity (Cellini, 1995). Cellini recounts, for example, how at the age of nineteen he and a woodcarver named Tasso decided on a whim to leave Florence for Rome. The two immediately set out walking until, near Siena, Tasso complained of sore feet and begged Cellini for the money he needed to return home. The artist persuaded his friend to carry on and they did, laughing and singing as they walked.

Once he had established himself as a leading artist, Cellini was able to travel in greater style, returning to Florence with 'plenty of money, a fellow to wait on me, and a good horse' (Cellini, 1995: 73). But even then, he still rubbed shoulders with a range of other mobile people en route, especially in spaces such as rural inns and ferry stations. For instance, Cellini mentions several encounters with couriers, the cavalrymen of the expanding postal service and thus an increasingly ubiquitous presence on Renaissance roads. One courier tried to borrow money from the artist at a mountain inn before they travelled on together towards Lyon; another Cellini met on the way to Bologna and again they continued on in company to Ferrara and then to Venice by boat. Cellini's *Vita* reminds us too how all travellers could face risks and dangers on the road, as when he describes in dramatic detail how two horses in his party slipped off a precipitous mountain path as they made their way through the Alps on the way to France.[7]

The *Vita* is just one of many sources offering precious details about the practical aspects of moving in the Renaissance, as well as the social and professional interactions that mobility entailed. Such testimonies also reveal how a broad constellation of more or less permanent and more or less official sites – roads, bridges, quays, inns, hostels, lodging houses, border checkpoints, customs houses, post and quarantine stations – sustained, directed, and sometimes impeded movement in this period. Using such evidence to shine a light onto the spaces and systems which underpinned mobility helps us to better understand the experience of being on the move and the factors that moulded and constrained it. It also reminds us of the imprint that seemingly ephemeral flows of people and things left on urban and rural landscapes and built environments.

Casting a close eye on some of the spaces in which people passed the time moving (or waiting to move) is a crucial step towards unpicking the practice and significance of Renaissance mobility. This approach can tell us about the

---

[7] For more on the impact of mobility on the style of Renaissance artists such as Cellini, see Young Kim (2014). On couriers, see Section 3.

interactions between different kinds of travellers and between travellers and locals, as well as about the tensions between individual agency and larger institutional structures. More broadly, a focus on infrastructures and spaces exposes the practical and material contexts in which mobility was enacted. This section considers some of the infrastructures that supported and shaped Renaissance mobility – especially those of hospitality, transport, and control – while also highlighting how those infrastructures intertwined, reinforced, and sometimes hindered each other.

1.1 Transport

Renaissance journeys frequently made use of transport infrastructure laid down in earlier centuries. This infrastructure, a product of the expansion of trade and urbanization in the late Middle Ages, included an extensive road network (reviving in some instances arteries that had fallen into decline along with the Roman Empire), river and shipping systems, and new mountain passes through the Alps (Verdon, 2003: chap. 1).[8] The consolidation of these routes allowed more and more people to travel more frequently and over longer distances: merchants expanding trading networks; artisans learning, practicing, and passing on craft skills; students and scholars frequenting the new universities; pilgrims travelling to the Holy Land or other sacred sites in Europe; and diplomats forging connections between different states. By the fifteenth century, such voluntary migrants were joined ever more frequently by many others forced onto the road because of war, poverty, enslavement, or religious persecution.

Whatever the reason for setting out, *how* a person travelled communicated a great deal about their identity and status. A stranger appearing in a new place on foot was treated very differently from one who arrived on a horse or in a coach. Clothing, baggage, and retinue were other important determinants of reception. Nonetheless, travelling on foot remained the most common mode of moving, even over very long distances. Only between one-quarter and one-third of arrivals to Bologna in the fourteenth century, for example, came on horseback (Coulet, 1982: 201). Pedestrian travellers had little to protect them from bad weather conditions and other dangers and yet still might cover ten to thirty kilometres per day. Aside from the young Cellini and his companion Tasso, they ranged from the likes of Martin Luther (who in 1510 made a round trip on foot from Erfurt to Rome, 750 miles each way) and Ignatius Loyola (who walked from the Netherlands to Spain and across Italy) to vagrants on the move or peasants selling their produce.

---

[8] On the maintenance of roads, see Geltner (2019).

The wealthy and powerful could move faster, in greater comfort, and with fewer obstructions, somewhat like today's 'kinetic elite' (Urry, 2007: 152). Throughout the Renaissance period, however, there were various improvements in the ease, speed, and reliability of transport which opened up more options to less affluent passengers. From the sixteenth century, coaches and carriages proliferated, making moving much easier especially for those for whom horseback travel was inadvisable for reasons of health or propriety (including the young, the old, women, and clergymen). These conveyances moved along an expanding network of postal routes and stations offering fresh horses for hire. River transport also became easier, cheaper, and more commonly used for passengers rather than only for transporting goods, while sleds or sedan chairs might be employed to carry passengers in particularly challenging conditions or at certain times of year (Scott, 2015).

Well-traversed parts of Europe saw improvements in coordination between different forms of transport, so that travellers at key nodal points could transfer more seamlessly from one means to another. For example, it was customary to leave one's horses on the Italian mainland before continuing on to the major hub of Venice by boat, as in 1514 when a Hungarian envoy deposited his steeds at an inn in Treviso so that he could make a brief trip into the lagoon city, intending to collect them on the way back (Sanudo, 1879–1903: XIX, col. 437). At the edge of the Venetian lagoon, an ingenious device called the *carro*, patented by a French inventor in the fifteenth century, transferred river boats into the lagoon. While this novel technology facilitated access to the city, it also benefitted a local noble family who earned a tidy sum from their licence to collect tolls and rent out the adjacent inn (Molà, 2010).

Despite many advances, moving still meant facing numerous risks and obstacles, as we saw in the case of Cellini. Leaving the relative safety of a city for the countryside aroused fears of attack by wild beasts such as wolves or of injuries sustained falling from a horse or cart. Travellers often moved in groups for safety or had to change course because of the rumour of bandits ahead. Wealthier people could afford to hire experienced guides and drivers to accompany them through dangerous or difficult terrain. Those who moved on foot and had fewer resources may have had less to lose but were nonetheless more vulnerable to adversity. The Venetian pilgrim Bartolomeo Fontana, on his way to Santiago de Compostela in Spain, altered his itinerary several times after hearing word of famine ahead. Crossing the St Gotthard pass in the Alps, Fontana confronted a terrifying blizzard but was saved by a local girl who spoke Italian and accompanied him safely to an inn. On another occasion, the pilgrim lost his way in a violent storm and was forced to sleep outside covered only by his mantle (Fontana, 1995).

Sea travel was likewise undertaken at considerable risk of disease or death and continued to inspire great fear. Assault by pirates or other enemies was another danger and could provoke delays or changes of course. As on the road, weather was a frequent impediment to progress: both lack of wind and bad weather could prolong a journey. On board boats and ships conditions were challenging, even for wealthier passengers. Although those with greater means could choose a better, more private cabin, the Bruges merchant Anselme Adorno, who made a pilgrimage to Jerusalem in the fifteenth century, complained of the cramped conditions and the spread of disease on board Venetian galleys, while the German pilgrim Felix Fabri recounted in lurid terms the habitual stench of urine and vomit on these vessels (Verdon, 2003: 87–9; Arbel, 2017).

As well as discomfort and danger, even more affluent travellers could not insulate themselves entirely from other people, including those of vastly different status or background. The French nobleman and writer Michel de Montaigne, travelling through Italy on horseback in the early 1580s, encountered peasants peddling strawberries, soldiers begging on the roads, and artisans selling candles, images, and beads on the way to the shrine at Loreto (Montaigne, 2003). Carriages and riverboats could also be spaces of social mixing, in terms of both class and gender. On the boats which day and night plied the Brenta canal from Padua to Venice, travellers remarked on the mixture of passengers. The Englishman Fynes Moryson noted that 'commonly there is pleasant discourse, and the prouerb saith, that the boat shall bee drowned, when it carries neither Monke, nor Student, nor Curtesan . . . the passengers being for the most part of these kindes' (Moryson, 1617: I, 74–5).

Long journeys in confined spaces necessitated even more interaction with fellow passengers (and crew), and indeed ships in this period have been described as 'temporary microcosm[s]' or 'small world[s] afloat' (Arbel, 2017; see also Sardelic, 2022). Europeans motivated to move for religious reasons, both men and some women, might travel alongside merchants on commercial voyages, soldiers, or magistrates going to administer distant colonies, not to mention the multilingual (and multifaith) crews of sailors recruited from different ports. Despite this diversity, some kind of fleeting, fragile community could take shape as people passed the time on board with conversations, meals, games, or music making.

To be sure, effort was made to maintain distances and enforce hierarchies between passengers of different sex, class, race, and religion, at least as much as the confined space of the ship allowed. Fynes Moryson recounts how, on the ship which carried him to the Levant in 1596, Orthodox Greeks, Italian Catholics, and northern European Protestants like himself were allowed to pray silently up on deck according to their own faiths, while Turks, Persians, and Indians went 'under the hatches' to follow their devotional rituals (1617: I, 210). Yet this example also points towards some degree of cross-cultural and interfaith co-existence, even if conflicts still arose. As one late-sixteenth-century German pilgrim advised, 'all travellers should avoid arguments about matters of belief with any Turk, Jew, Greek, Armenian or any other such people who might happen also to be on board, and should do nothing to vex them' (cited in Sardelic, 2022: 29).

In addition to on-board encounters, further interactions took place during frequent stops at ports along the way, to restock with supplies such as food and water, or from smaller boats which approached the ship to trade or to inspect it. Arrival at a destination would inevitably bring about a whole new range of exchanges. The merchant R'ad from Aleppo, for example, describes sailing into the Venetian lagoon in the mid-seventeenth century where his galley was greeted by friendly cannon fire, followed by a cautious interaction with local officials who took letters from the ship's captain with a pair of tweezers and dipped them in vinegar before reading them for fear that they carried plague, then accompanied the crew to the Lazzaretto to complete their period of quarantine (Pedani & Issa, 2016: 393–4).

Whether they were ports where people arrived by boat or ship or were landlocked conurbations reached on foot or by horse, mule, or carriage, cities across Europe were crucial hubs of transport and other mobility infrastructures. The original location of urban centres had generally been determined by proximity to roads and waterways, their shape and appearance conditioned over the centuries by the need to enable but also to control movement in and out via architectural structures such as gates, walls, and quays (Gonzalez Martin, Salzberg & Zenobi, 2021; Nevola, 2021). Renaissance cities continued to be critical sites of gathering and exchange, shaped by ebbs and flows of movement, both long-range and short-distance, habitual and extraordinary (Calabi & Christensen, 2007). The influx of pilgrims in a jubilee year, merchants for annual trade fairs, or soldiers on campaign, for example, could temporarily change the culture and complexion of an urban community. Over the period, cities like London, Naples, or Lisbon grappled with the challenges of becoming ever larger and more diverse metropolises thanks to a rising tide of inward migration (De Munck & Winter, 2012; Gschwend & Lowe, 2015). But city life also continued to be underpinned by constant, smaller-scale movements in and out from the surrounding areas, such as peasants transporting produce to sell or coming into town to attend religious festivities (Hewlett, 2016).

1.2 Hospitality

Having arrived at a new place, whether stopping briefly or intending to linger or even to settle, the most important next question was usually where to stay. As with the choice of transport, where one stayed often depended on factors such as wealth, status, religion, provenance, and purpose for moving. At the very top of the social scale, eminent arrivals such as ambassadors and other visiting dignitaries could expect a warm welcome. Urban authorities usually prepared palaces for their use and billeted their servants and followers with local families or in inns (Heal, 1990; Goldstein & Piana, 2021). Migrants or travellers with friends or family at their destination might expect to be hosted by them, while workers sometimes lodged with their employers, at least for a brief period. The very poorest and most 'friendless' arrivals could be forced to sleep rough, under porticoes or in piazzas. But many others looked to an infrastructure of hospitality – both charitable and commercial – that had emerged in the Middle Ages to cater to different groups of people on the move and that, once again, became more extensive and variegated in the Renaissance period.

Ancient and Medieval ideas of charitable or non-commercial hospitality – accommodating a visitor without expectation of a material recompense – persisted throughout the Renaissance. Poor or sick travellers might be hosted for free, at least for a few nights, in accordance with the Christian (and also Jewish) duty to offer hospitality to strangers in need (Constable, 2006; Healy, 2007).[9] From the Middle Ages, hospitals and hostels to shelter travellers en route proliferated in and around cities along major pilgrimage arteries (Henderson, 2006). For example, European pilgrims passing through Venice on their way to the Holy Land could find accommodation in one of ten or so dedicated hostels, such as the state-run Ospedale dei Pellegrini with its thirty-five beds (Semi, 1983). New institutions also were founded in the Renaissance to treat the sick poor who increasingly flocked into urban centres for treatment (Henderson, 2006).[10] Most charitable hospitality, however, whether offered by community organizations, local authorities, or benevolent individuals, exercised discernment and was aimed at particular groups. In Rome from the thirteenth century, for instance, Armenian Christians made their way to their dedicated hospice near St Peter's, where they were given a bed (in a common dorm room, unless they were a high cleric or noble), bed linen, and a small allowance to permit

---

[9] See also Ebrahim (2021) on Muslim charitable hospitality towards travellers in the Ottoman Empire.

[10] On the reform of poor relief across Europe in this period, which increasingly involved housing local indigent people in institutions – and thereby preventing them from wandering around and begging – but also expelling foreign poor, see Jütte (1994); Hitchcock (2020).

them to feed themselves during their stay in the Eternal City and to help with their onward journey (Santus, 2019).[11]

For the many people who moved for more humble forms of work, designated establishments set up by colleagues or compatriots made the task of finding accommodation easier. Tramping artisans, for example, often stayed in hostels established by their fellow workers (who might also hail from the same town or region), as in the case of the German shoemakers in Venice (Braunstein, 2016: 659; see also Kümin, 2007: 22–3). The artist Federico Zuccaro, who came from a small town in the Marche region, made provisions in his will to establish a *foresteria* to house young artists who moved to Rome (Young Kim, 2014: 219). From the perspective of local authorities, such structures might also serve a useful function in concentrating and controlling the presence of foreign workers in town, at least temporarily. In Frankfurt-am-Main, every journeyman entering the city was required to go directly to his *Gesellenherberge* (a lodging house for his own guild) where he was usually allowed to stay no more than eight days while looking for employment (Kamp, 2018).

The desire to protect but also to closely monitor the foreign presence also spurred some civic leaders to encourage or indeed command that merchants belonging to certain national or religious groups lodge together in designated spaces. In Europe, the late Middle Ages saw the adaptation of the *funduq* model from the Muslim world, first in parts of Spain and Sicily and later, famously, in great trading centres such as Venice. These urban compounds offered room for foreign merchants to comfortably sleep, socialize, eat familiar foods, and practise their faith but also to conduct their business under the watchful eye of the local authorities, who taxed each transaction (Constable, 2006). Elsewhere in Europe, visiting merchants clustered in particular neighbourhoods, or nominated hostels or inns, where they could store and display their goods and conclude deals but also be supervised by government officials and the innkeepers charged with reporting their comings and goings (Peyer, 2009: 152–3, 240–1; Harreld, 2003). *Fondaci* and merchant hostels constituted points of gathering for the wider community of compatriot travellers and migrants. When he arrived in Venice, for instance, the pilgrim Felix Fabri went first to the German merchants' trading house (the Fondaco dei Tedeschi) near Rialto to gather news from home and a recommendation for a good local inn (Constable, 2006: 318).

---

[11] Apart from religiously motivated charity, other reasons also compelled individuals to host needy travellers. For example, Martin Crusius, professor of Greek at Tübingen University in the sixteenth century, was spurred by his intellectual curiosity to offer free lodging to a series of eastern Christian Orthodox mendicant priests, hoping to learn about their homeland and to improve his Greek (Calis, 2019).

As this last example indicates, people on the move in the Renaissance were able to choose from an expanding range of commercial accommodation options. The mobility of certain groups such as merchants and pilgrims in earlier centuries had laid the groundwork for an increasingly sophisticated infrastructure of commercial hospitality that would cater to an ever-wider range of mobile people, including proto-tourists (Davis & Marvin, 2004: 17). Broadly speaking, the Renaissance saw the continuation of the trend by which the commercial hospitality sector expanded and began to overtake other forms of accommodation provision. While venues such as inns and lodging houses started out as basic support for economic activities such as trade, often with lordly, communal, or governmental impetus or at least close oversight, they developed ever more into an important economic sector in their own right, employing large numbers of people (Peyer, 2009).

Inns were especially lucrative sources of income both for governmental coffers (usually via a wine tax) and for their owners (often elite families or ecclesiastical establishments), who rented them out to innkeepers. As mentioned, they could also be commandeered to house visiting diplomats and aristocratic entourages, as well as lower-level functionaries such as messengers bringing news from foreign states or army officers on their way to the battlefield (Tuliani, 1994: 163; Kümin, 2007: 128; Salzberg, 2021). The pope himself bore the expense of lodging Holy Roman Emperor Frederick III and his retinue of 700 men and horses in around twenty Roman inns in 1468–9, while a few decades later Duke Gian Galeazzo Sforza ordered that the Venetian ambassadors be lodged in luxurious rooms at the inn of the Three Kings in Milan, where they were greeted by servants and musicians upon arrival (Zaniboni, 1921: 120; Motta, 1898: 374).

In the Medieval period, various kinds of commercial hospitality establishments (inns, taverns, alehouses, etc.) offering accommodation, food, and drink to people on the move had grown up, especially along commercial routes and near important destinations such as churches, monasteries, castles, courts, and ports. Increasingly, travellers were likely to find them at strategic intervals on the main roads along which they progressed as well as in urban centres near key sites like marketplaces and government buildings. These 'public houses' also tended to cluster close to the walls or just inside or outside the gates of cities – as in the case of the nine inns found along the road approaching Toledo from Madrid in the sixteenth century – along with other businesses serving people on the move such as farriers and coachmakers (Gobel, 2018; cf. Tuliani, 1994; Modigliani, 1999). By the early modern period, some cities hosted an impressive number and range of establishments, although it can be difficult to compare the scale of urban commercial hospitality infrastructures because of differences in terminology and classification. One estimate suggests there was typically one public house per 200 to 500 inhabitants (Peyer, 2009: 286); in Bavaria in 1580, for instance, there was one for every 471 people (Kümin, 2007: 26).

In both larger cities and more rural areas, Renaissance travellers could identify a likely inn, whether by means of its sign (which might consist of a cloth or a wreath of leaves hung on a pole or a protruding image such as a saint, an animal, or an astrological sign painted or sculpted [Figure 2]) or by the telltale sounds of clinking glasses, music, and conversation. Newcomers might also be lured by innkeepers in spaces of transit or transport, such as at city gates or on boats approaching the centre, despite prohibitions against this kind of aggressive advertisement in many places (Zaniboni, 1921: 57; Romani, 1948: 112). As in the case of the German pilgrim Fabri, the choice of inn might be determined by word-of-mouth recommendations from compatriots. Elsewhere, travellers of the same religion were compelled by local authorities to stay in a particular locale. Such was the case, for example, with the inns in which Jewish travellers were required to lodge in cities like Siena or Venice (Tuliani, 1994: 177; Costantini, 1996: 904).

Figure 2 Drawing by Hans Bol of a covered wagon arriving at a village with two inns, identified by their protruding signs, 1580. Victoria and Albert Museum, London.

Aside from public inns, much remains to be known about the broader 'shadow' economy of lodging in private houses, a practice which governing authorities across Europe increasingly tried to regulate in this period for both fiscal and security reasons. Although harder to study because of its often unofficial nature, this custom undoubtedly supplied accommodation to large numbers of people on the move and to new arrivals to cities, particularly groups such as artisans and sailors on shore leave. It was especially important during moments of particular influx, as in Rome during jubilee years, when the city was overrun with pilgrims, or in Frankfurt during the annual trade fairs (Romani, 1948; Coulet, 1982; Canepari, 2014; Salzberg, 2019). From the seventeenth century, ever more rapid urbanization saw the burgeoning of lodging sectors in European cities such as London and Paris, especially with the need to house growing numbers of rural-to-urban migrants (Roche, 2000).[12]

Lodging houses may have been especially appealing to female migrants and travellers since, in some places at least, it was not considered appropriate for women to stay in inns, where the proximity to unknown men and insalubrious activities such as prostitution, excessive drinking, and gambling might compromise reputations. It was for this reason that a citizen from Trogir in Dalmatia travelling with his wife, his female cousin, and her infant daughter, plus a wet nurse, sought permission, in Venice in 1530, to stay in a lodging house rather than an inn.[13]

While such a choice was possible in a large metropolis like Venice, in rural areas travellers generally had fewer options about where to stay. Rural inns were quintessential spaces of encounter between very different types of people. In the words of the highly mobile humanist Erasmus of Rotterdam (1466–1536), their clientele might include 'travellers on foot, horsemen, traders, sailors, carriers, farmers, youths, women, the sick and the whole' (Erasmus, 1997: 371). Heiss, citing the example of a sixteenth-century Tyrolean inn that hosted the Holy Roman Emperor and then a few days later accommodated farmers sleeping on straw, argues that 'no other social arena surpassed the public house's quality of encompassing all classes – not even the local church' (2002: 167).

If the long-term trend was towards increasing privacy and comfort for more affluent travellers, sharing space nonetheless remained a common experience. Eating together in common rooms or at common tables was the norm in many inns and lodging houses; in the same colloquy by Erasmus just quoted, a character describes having to undress and change his wet underwear alongside other guests in the communal space of a German inn (Erasmus, 1997: 371).

---

[12] For more on lodging-house keepers, who were often women, see Section III.

[13] Archivio di stato, Venice, Giustizia Nuova, busta 5, registro 12, fol. 11v. Cf. Canepari (2013). On different gendered experiences of mobility in this period, see also Section II.

Sharing a bed was also not uncommon, especially in rural areas, where there were fewer accommodation options. Boccaccio's *Decameron* includes a famous tale of bed-sharing and bed-hopping set in a small inn outside Florence where the guests occupied one bedroom along with the host and his family (Boccaccio, 2012: 507–10). In a later example, a Dutch pilgrim on his way to Santiago de Compostela in the late fifteenth century described how he and his travelling companion took revenge for the poor accommodation offered them at an inn by urinating into their shared bed so that it ran through the floor to the room of the innkeeper and his wife below (cited in Cohen, 2021: 313–14). Even those who could pay for the most expensive accommodation were likely to share their room (possibly even their bed) with travel companions. Urban inn inventories show that a great many bedrooms included one or more low truckle beds, probably stored under larger bedsteads and wheeled out to be slept on by servants or less prestigious members of travelling groups (Salzberg, 2021).

Nonetheless, the period did see the enhancement of accommodation provision in many places, offering ever higher levels of luxury and comfort to those who could afford it. Cities with a large number of different hospitality sites – such as Rome or Venice – were more likely to provide a range of options suiting clientele with different means and requirements. High-quality provision also was increasingly closely linked to contemporary improvements in communication and transport infrastructure, with better inns constructed along the routes of the developing postal system (Susini, 2018). Travel diaries and other sources document the increasing material comfort to be found in some Renaissance inns. Although the material conditions of mobility will be considered more closely in the next section, suffice to say that travellers of means could expect more space and privacy in their sleeping accommodations, tighter security for their person and belongings, higher quality linens and bedding, and more elaborate furniture and decoration (beyond just beds, tables, and chairs, also increasingly paintings, carpets, wall hangings, and much else), as well as better food and wine (Fanfani, 1936; Tuliani, 1994; Kümin, 2007).

Inns did not just provide for travellers' most basic needs. They were also 'pillars of pre-modern travel infrastructure, providers of indispensable services and venues of the most varied kinds of social exchange' (Kümin & Tlusty, 2011: II, 290).[14] They performed numerous economic functions, including providing space for business meetings and trade deals, the storage and display of merchandise, or the recruitment of workers. Renaissance inns also hosted a variety of other activities – from magistrates' courts and auctions to wedding feasts and

---

[14] For more on the role of innkeepers in facilitating various types of commercial, cultural, and social exchange, see Section III.

public dances – that might have the added function of exposing visitors and new arrivals to local community life (Coulet, 1982; Kümin, 2007). Passing the time waiting for the next stage of a journey or in between conducting business or seeking a job, guests might be distracted and diverted by the pleasant conversation, jokes, and stories of innkeepers and their staff, as well as by a great variety of musical or theatrical performances. Stopping at the Osteria della Rosa in the border city of Trento between Italy and the Holy Roman Empire on their way north, for example, some Venetian diplomats witnessed a buffoon and a girl playing a stringed instrument and singing songs in German for the mostly northern European clientele (Simonsfield, 1903: 284). In Italy, Montaigne noted that 'you find rhymers in almost all the hostelries who make rhymes on the spot, suitable for the persons present' (2003: 1191). In England and Spain, inns, particularly large ones with suitable courtyards, might act as playhouses (Hunter, 2002: 79; Gobel, 2018). 'Monsters' and marvels could also be witnessed, as they were carried around from place to place and put on display. The Venetian diarist Sanudo recorded how he had entered the Cappello inn off Piazza San Marco – attracted by an advertising banner outside – to witness a 'monstrous' boy from France with two torsos and heads who had been brought to the city and exhibited to paying customers by some entrepreneurial Spaniards (1879–1903: II, col. 179). Crucially, too, entertainment at inns often included sex: prostitutes were habitual patrons of public houses, where they met with potential clients both local and foreign.

Related to both the economic and the entertainment functions of inns was their role as vital enablers of communication both face-to-face and long-distance. As well as providing physical staging posts for horse-mounted couriers and later for coaches, forming the nodes on the expanding postal network, they supplied space for the more ephemeral conversations of customers and guests who met to gossip, debate, and discuss, to sell and consume books, ballads, and newsletters, and sometimes even to plan conspiracies and uprisings (Kümin, 2007: 127–8; Pettegree, 2014: chap. 6). Because of this capacity as information hubs local authorities used inns to communicate with their subjects and citizens (circulating copies of laws and regulations there), as well as with visitors. In Ferrara, for example, the bedroom doors at one inn displayed signs reminding travellers to 'Remember your health certificate' and to report to the local authorities immediately after arrival (Montaigne, 2003: 1129).

Inns and other hospitality sites were ever more frequent targets of official control. This was a result of the numerous activities that took place in them and also simply because they hosted foreigners whom local authorities wished to monitor. To prevent violence and disturbances to morality and public order, and often to limit the contact between local clientele and visitors, there were normally strict rules about their opening and closing times: usually only over-night guests could remain after a certain hour. Throughout this period, inns also became an increasingly important part of the infrastructure for monitoring and registering the presence and movements of foreigners on behalf of state and urban governments. From at least the fourteenth century, innkeepers in cities like Bologna, Siena, and Florence had to submit daily lists of their guests' arrivals and departures to the authorities. From the fifteenth century, many northern European cities followed suit (Tuliani, 1994: 74; Romani, 1948: 166; Hell, 2014; Peyer, 2009: 253–4; Kamp, 2018).

Such regulations made inns very useful points of surveillance. Indeed, when the artist Michelangelo tried to stay in Ferrara incognito, his presence was quickly discovered thanks to Duke Alfonso I d'Este's scrutiny of the guest records of the city's inns. Wanting the artist to work for him, the duke immedi-ately sent for Michelangelo to be moved to a more luxurious palace (Vasari, 1912–15: IX, 48). For this very reason, people who needed to keep a low profile for one reason or another might eschew public inns, as in the case of a group of forcibly converted Jews, escaped from Portugal and on their way from Antwerp towards Italy in the 1540s, who chose to sleep on a boat on the Rhine instead of in an inn, for fear of discovery (Mazzei, 2013: 173).

1.3 Control

Such examples illustrate how a large-scale infrastructure of control over the movement of people was permeating even the interior spaces of commercial hospitality establishments in the Renaissance. And indeed, this era was marked by the expansion of systems of surveillance and restriction of movement that went beyond the traditional built structures of earlier centuries (typically walls and gates) to encompass newer spaces (such as quarantine stations, inns, and customs points) and practices (particularly the use of documentary identifica-tion and registration). Even as city gates and walls retained a significant role for some time as convenient points to control people on the move – the forerunners of modern airport or border checkpoints – at the same time these urban border spaces became more closely linked into broader (regional or state-level) infra-structures for controlling mobility (Greefs & Winter, 2018).

Entering a Renaissance city by land usually meant having to pass through walls via a gate, as one can see in the image of Nuremberg from the late fifteenth century shown in Figure 3. For the arrival of important persons, this might be the occasion for carefully staged ceremonial welcomes, including music and pageantry. But for most people the act of entry was a 'complex and often multistage process' (Jütte, 2014: 218) whereby travellers of all kinds could be

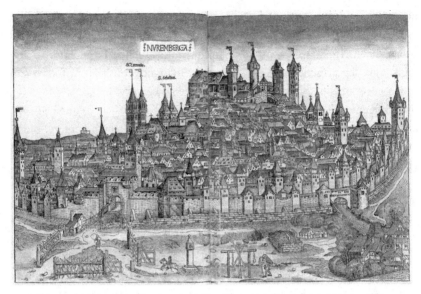

Figure 3 Woodcut of Nuremberg from Hartmann Schedel, *Nuremberg Chronicle* (Nuremberg: Anton Koberger, 1493), showing the city walls and a gate, with people arriving on foot and on horseback. Wikimedia Commons (CC BY 4.0).

examined both physically and verbally: asked where they came from, what their purpose was, how long they intended to stay. In some places they had to surrender any weapons they carried, pay tolls, have their baggage inspected, and present identification documents. This allowed gates to function as a kind of 'social filter', used to prevent unwanted arrivals, especially as Renaissance authorities became increasingly intolerant of foreign beggars and vagabonds who, it was feared, would prove a burden on local resources, cause disorder, or import disease (Jütte, 2014; see also Boes, 2007; Coy, 2008; De Munck & Winter, 2012). Whether to admit a person – and what kind of welcome that person received – depended on numerous factors, from their clothing to their form of transport, the possession (or lack) of passports, safe conduct letters, and other documents from authorities, or indeed their ability to bribe the guards.

Gates also regulated flows of traffic by closing at night, determining rhythms of traffic and mobility. While some cities boasted ingenious mechanisms to filter the flow of people at the gates, such as a famously elaborate gate at Augsburg (described by Montaigne, 2003: 1099–1100), the crucial role of surveillance and control of people and goods moving in and out was entrusted mostly to gatekeepers and other low-level officials. Entering Rome, for example, Montaigne complained that his belongings were examined 'right down to the smallest articles' and his books confiscated (although they were returned to him as he left the city) (2003: 1143). He compared this experience to more perfunctory examinations on entering other Italian cities. Once strangers were granted entry, they might be given a slip (in Italy known as a *bolletta*) which then had to be presented to the innkeeper at the place where they sought accommodation and shown again at the gates when leaving the city, so that individual arrivals and departures could be tracked (Jütte, 2014: 217; Tlusty, 2001: 22–4, 166–7). When records survive, such practices of mobility control give us a documentary snapshot, sometimes of great precision, of the numbers of people on the move in this period: for instance, 844 entered Bologna in a single month in 1412, 587 of them travelling alone and 218 with one or more companions (Saletti, 2017).[15] In Venice, encircled by its protective lagoon instead of walls, it was the boatmen ferrying people in and out the city who acted as de facto gatekeepers, supported by officials stationed at key points of embarkation and also hospitality providers in the urban centre. Ferry operators had to inform arrivals about local laws and regulations, prevent the passage of people suspected of carrying disease into the city, or indeed expel and deport unwanted migrants such as beggars, vagabonds, or foreign prostitutes (Quillien & Rivoal, 2020).

Nonetheless, despite increased sophistication in the surveillance of mobile people, such systems were far from watertight. Sometimes, as in Stockholm well into the early modern period, the urban 'walls' were in some places little more than hoardings or fences that could be slipped through quite easily (even if an illegal entrant might then be picked up in the city by some of the other forms of monitoring just described) (Sennefelt, 2018). Even when Florence was supposedly sealed off by a *cordon sanitaire* in 1630 to try to prevent the arrival of plague, the authorities worried that people were managing to slip in and out when the gates were left open or by pretending to bathe in the Arno river (Henderson, 2019: 30–1). As well as such physical loopholes, Fynes Moryson also reminds us that even the most advanced bureaucratic systems of the period had their limits. In Venice, the Englishman noted that 'no stranger may lie in the City more then a night, without leaue of the Magistrates appointed for that purpose'. 'But,' he added, 'the next day telling them some pretended causes of your comming to the Towne, they will easily grant you leaue to stay longer, and after that you shall be no more troubled, how long soeuer you stay, onely your Host after certaine daies giueth them account of you' (Moryson, 1617: I, 90).

We see a similar development of control mechanisms across rural areas in this period. However, these were more likely to be located on key transit corridors,

---

[15] See also the less complete records of arrivals, by land and sea, to Ragusa in 1500–30, discussed in Blazina Tomic and Blazina (2015): chap. 5.

at crossing points such as roads and rivers, rather than at the frontiers between different states. Scholz argues that while political boundaries 'feature prominently' on contemporary maps in areas such as the Holy Roman Empire, 'they did not pose a particular obstacle to most travellers until the mid-eighteenth century', adding that 'the conception of pre-modern borders as closable membranes is at odds with the experience of mobile populations during much of the early modern period' (2020: 127). At the same time, ordinary people were aware of the sites and mechanisms that controlled mobility and might engage actively and knowledgeably with them, as in the case of the numerous soldiers, exiles, and small-time traders and transporters who petitioned for safe conducts to move across the border between the states of Milan and Venice in the fifteenth century. Between 1452 and 1465 the Milanese chancery issued at least 2000 such documents, at a rate of one every three or four days (Zenobi, 2018).

Many of the new spaces and mechanisms for controlling mobility introduced in this period were spurred by the effort to contain the spread of epidemic diseases, especially in the wake of the devastating Black Death of the fourteenth century, which itself was followed by frequently recurring, if less lethal, bouts of plague. Particularly vulnerable to the spread of disease because of its position as a shipping nexus between the Italian peninsula and the Ottoman Empire, the city-state of Ragusa (now Dubrovnik), for example, pioneered the use of quarantine from at least 1377. Arrivals from places suspected of harbouring plague henceforth were to be isolated on an island just outside the city for one month before they could enter (Blazina Tomic & Blazina, 2015). Northern Italian cities such as Milan and Venice – similarly at great risk as major hubs of trade and transit – followed this model and soon also developed other innovative and influential policies. These included travel bans on those coming from infected places during periods of epidemic and other practices that allowed mobility and thus trade to continue while diminishing the threat of disease (Stevens Crawshaw, 2015). In practice, such policies could represent a severe hindrance for travellers, as the humanist publisher Aldus Manutius found in 1506 when he was briefly thrown in jail on suspicion of violating such a ban by journeying from Venice to Mantua; he was only released after he appealed to the Mantuan Duke Francesco Gonzaga (Minuzzi, 2020: 25–7).

After establishing the world's first permanent plague hospital (the Lazzaretto Vecchio) in 1423, the Venetians in 1471 set up the Lazzaretto Nuovo on another island in the lagoon as a space for the quarantine of people and the disinfection of goods. The walls of this Lazzaretto are still covered with graffiti (Figure 4) recording the passage through this structure of ships and their crews from all over the Adriatic and Mediterranean, as well as the smaller-scale mobility of *bastazi* or porters, mostly migrants from the mountains north of Venice, whose

Figure 4 Wall graffiti depicting a ship arrived from Constantinople, dated to the sixteenth or seventeenth century, in the Lazzaretto Nuovo, Venice. Photo author's own.

job it was to disinfect the quarantined merchandise (Malagnini, 2017). Lazzaretti for the confinement of travellers suspected of plague subsequently became a common feature not only of towns throughout the Venetian empire (including Verona, Bergamo, Brescia, Split, and Corfu) but also across northern Italy and later in other parts of Europe. These structures could be as much about facilitating the continued flow of (especially commercial) travellers and their goods as about confining and treating the sick (Stevens Crawshaw, 2015; Inì, 2021; Bilic, 2023).

Efforts to control disease also led Italians to pioneer the development of various forms of documentary identification for people on the move, among them the increasingly ubiquitous health passes or *bollettini di sanità*. First handwritten and later printed on small slips that could be filled in with

Figure 5 Health pass issued by the health officials of Bologna, 1632, for a traveller from Prato accompanied by his servant and two horses. The Wellcome Collection. Public Domain Mark.

individual details (such as in the example from seventeenth-century Bologna in Figure 5), these became increasingly common from the later fifteenth century (Bamji, 2019). The use of safe conducts and, from the sixteenth century, passports also became more frequent throughout the period and more widespread across the continent, as a way for local and state authorities to permit the movement of goods and people (Nordman, 1987; Groebner, 2007). Increasingly states and localities worked with each other to synchronize their controls on the itineraries and identification of mobile people. In Bologna, for example, relevant decrees, notifications, and forms from neighbouring states were collected by the local health office so that information could be shared across borders, for example about which places were subject to a travel ban in times of plague or how to discern the difference between authentic and forged identification documents (Carnevali, 2020).

And yet, even as print began to be used to standardize forms of documentary identification and states' efforts became more coordinated, the regulation of mobility remained a highly contingent practice. Travellers who were seen to pose a particular threat (whether religious, social, or epidemiological) were always likely to face greater impediments to movement and much more scrutiny along the way. Fear about the spread of disease was hard to disentangle from anxieties about other kinds of undesirable mobilities. The mobile poor (such as beggars and vagrants) were particularly suspected as carriers of disease, and many restrictions on movement were targeted especially at them. At times, it was not so much a case of which document a person carried but of who it was who carried it; the most humble migrants might not be allowed into a city even when possessing the appropriate identification, whereas noble travellers might enter even without such identification, as their clothing, bearing, and means of transport communicated their status even more effectively (Kamp, 2018; Sennefelt, 2018). Ultimately, 'for everyone, mobility was something to be negotiated, often individually and at different levels' (Scholz, 2020: 9), if not with the highest levels of authority then with the bureaucrats who issued safe conduct passes or the guards at toll stations.

The creation of infrastructures of mobility has been integral to the development of states since the Renaissance and likely even earlier. As Quirk and Vigneswaran write, 'all states – historical and contemporary – have consistently made sustained efforts to legitimize, condition, discipline, and profit from human mobility … [T]hese efforts, successful or otherwise, have been of a sufficient scale and significance that it is necessary to treat mobility as a central factor when it comes to both the constitution and everyday operation of state authority' (2015: 6). One feature of Renaissance mobility was the increasing coordination of spaces and infrastructures of mobility from above and on supra-regional scales, connecting into each other and cooperating across jurisdictional lines to forge a more effective system. Such was the case with the development of the postal network which allowed for increasingly rapid communications as well as enabling faster and more regular transport and spurring the enhancement of hospitality sites along its routes.

At the same time, looking closely at how these infrastructures, systems, and spaces operated helps us to recount a history of mobility not just from the perspective of states. This history can be reconfigured by adopting different, and more versatile, perspectives, also taking into account the experiences and actions of the many people who made use of, passed through, managed, and maintained these infrastructures. I have suggested in this section how factors such as transport, hospitality, and mechanisms of control conditioned the paths of mobile people in vital ways, whether by blocking or enabling their movement, by making travel faster or slower and more or less comfortable, or by providing them with access to information or entertainment that eased the passage from one stage of a journey to the next. I have also illustrated how both mobile and fixed spaces, from boats and coaches to inns and gates, provided points where numerous people met and interacted – spaces which could not have functioned without the work of ordinary actors such as innkeepers and boatmen. Even if how, when, and whether a person moved depended very much on factors such as their status, gender, race, and religion, spaces of mobility remained sites where barriers could be broken down and encounters could be hard to avoid.

2 Materialities

In his account of his own journeys across Renaissance Europe and the Mediterranean in the 1590s, the English traveller Fynes Moryson checked off a range of physical and mental characteristics that could help a person confront the challenges of mobility.

> The Italians say in their tongue "a traveller needs these things: the eye of a falcon (to see far), the ears of an ass (to hear well), the face of a monkey (to be ready to laugh), the mouth of a pig (to eat everything), the shoulders of a camel (to carry heavy loads with patience), the legs of a deer (to flee from danger) and a big sack of money (because he who has money is treated like a lord)". (Moryson, 1617: II, 49)

And indeed, Moryson's *Itinerary* is replete with examples of the need for a person on the move in this period to possess sharp senses, physical fortitude, and a readiness to adapt to different customs and environments. Travelling by sea to the Levant, for instance, Moryson described how he sewed his money into his doublet to safeguard it from thieves. On several occasions he recounts donning alternative clothing and guises to protect himself on the road. More than once he dressed as a poor servant and was treated accordingly, seated at the 'lower end' of the communal dining table in an inn. Fearing hostility as an English Protestant, he presented himself as a Pole at the gate of the French city of Nancy and as a German when entering Spanish-run Milan, while in the Holy Land Moryson claimed to be Catholic in order to stay at a Franciscan convent. And he was not alone: at Voghera, in Lombardy, he encountered another Englishman trying to pass as a German but caught out his compatriot because of his poor command of that language (cf. Gallagher, 2023).

At the same time, Moryson also reminds us how financial resources ('a big sack of money') could have a very material impact on how someone fared on the road. As witnessed in the previous section, wealthier Renaissance travellers could opt for greater speed and comfort in transport and more space, privacy, and luxury in their choice of accommodation. The experience of moving was conditioned by a significant number of variables: whether one had the means to travel on horseback or in a carriage or was required to trudge along the road; stayed in a comfortable inn or slept in a stable; was welcomed with fanfare at city gates or brusquely turned away. Beyond some fundamental distinctions, however, we have also seen how mobility and its associated hardships could often also throw people together, with the effect of 'iron[ing] out social differences' to some degree (Maczak, 1995: 40). By the eighteenth century it would become increasingly possible for elite Europeans to travel in an enclosed bubble of luxury, separated from the masses on the move and with the comfort and space that allowed them to enjoy the passing landscape (Maudlin, 2020; see also Guldi, 2012). But this was by no means guaranteed in earlier centuries. While a person's status might affect their experience of mobility, at the same time it is evident that travel could blur numerous social distinctions. When people journeyed far from home and jostled for space on the road, in boats or carriages, or in inns and taverns, they were thrown together in surprising ways. Moreover, as Moryson shows, when travelling one might also choose, or be forced, to change one's clothes, disguise one's identity, eat different foods, and adopt new habits. Even the experience of shorter voyages had the capacity to break down barriers and erode social, religious, and political identities. Longer-term migration, on the other hand, led to more profound, incremental changes in people's habits and world views.

As well as questions of wealth, status, and religion, other factors such as age, race, and gender also had very significant effects on a person's mobility. Bodies were the one thing that everyone took with them when they moved, and mobility itself was an intensely embodied experience for all. Bodies were physically and emotionally marked by the act of moving and adapted in various ways to it. As such it is necessary to think about the materiality and physicality of being on the move in this period. How did different bodies move through space? What did it feel like to move? What things moved along with these bodies? What did people take with them to be able to rise to the challenges of changing place? In this section I explore these questions, looking at the changes that moving wrought on people's bodies, emotions, and identities in the Renaissance, as well as considering some of the items that people carried with them to assist their journeys.

2.1 Moving Bodies

Mobility in the Renaissance was recognized as an intense sensory experience, and generally more so the further one went from home. Sensations ranged from the intensely pleasurable to the frankly revolting. Travel diaries and other sources evoke the sensorial onslaught that moving inflicted on the body: 'wading through the mire' on dirty roads and streets; being forced to sleep outside in the cold when no other accommodation was available; enduring the stench of overturned chamber pots in the communal sleeping quarters of a crowded ship (Verhoeven, 2023; Arbel, 2017). The humanist Erasmus pungently evoked the 'belching of garlic, the breaking of wind, the stinking breaths' in an overcrowded German inn, where one feared catching some disease as all the guests inhaled the same warm air (1997: 371–2). The cacophony of a crowded metropolis – street sellers shouting, shop and tavernkeepers calling out to entice customers, animals and carts rattling by – also could be overwhelming, especially for the many rural migrants who arrived in cities to work or trade. If wealthier travellers found ways to insulate themselves from some of the less agreeable sensorial assaults associated with being on the move, they could not do so entirely. Even Niccolò Machiavelli, travelling as a diplomat to France to represent the Florentine Republic, complained of food poisoning, theft, and rats getting into his shoes in inns along the road (Benner, 2017: 245–9).

Beyond gradations of wealth and comfort, a crucial distinction was whether a person moved by choice or by force – the latter potentially in violent and appalling circumstances if we think of slaves crowded into the holds of ships and transported over vast distances. We can only imagine the experiences of enslaved people such as those from the Black Sea, 'sold by their wretched families to alleviate their hunger', described by the poet Petrarch as they were unloaded from ships at the port of fourteenth-century Venice (quoted in McKee, 2008: 305; see also Barker, 2019), or of Muslim captives processed through the streets of Renaissance cities in clanking chains or forced to do the back-breaking work of rowing Mediterranean galleys (Walden, 2020).

Another significant variable was whether those on the move had their belongings transported by someone else or had to carry them on their bodies, as in the case of the tramping peasant family – mother, father, and young child – depicted in an etching by Rembrandt (Figure 6).[16] Likewise, pedlars of printed items or haberdashery bore their merchandise in packs on their backs, even if the more successful members of this profession might be able to afford a mule or horse to convey their goods (Fontaine, 1996). As well as having their luggage carried, those with means could employ other people to smooth their journeys in numerous ways, such as one 'humble' Renaissance pilgrim who travelled to the Holy Land with a barber, a musician, a cook, and an interpreter (Arbel, 2017: 188). The affluent were likewise better able to protect their bodies from mortal risk, as in the case of the English gentleman John North who lodged safely on the mainland but sent his servant into Venice to fetch money for him when the city was being ravaged by a devastating plague in 1577 (Gallagher, 2017).

---

[16] Compare with Figure 1 in Section 1, an image of Arlecchino carrying his children on his back.

Figure 6 Rembrandt van Rijn, etching of a tramping peasant family carrying their belongings, ca. 1652. Minneapolis Institute of Art (CC BY 4.0).

Nonetheless, as these examples illustrate, Renaissance mobility was usually a collective experience. Whether migrating in search of work or on pilgrimage, fleeing danger or persecution, or seeking new experiences, people very often moved in groups. For reasons of safety and companionship, it was rare to venture out alone, especially on long journeys. An elite male heading a travelling party generally brought along an entourage of companions, servants, or family members, who shared the voyage even if they left few documentary traces of their feelings about it (Verhoeven, 2019). At the height of his success, for instance, the English adventurer Anthony Sherley travelled in style throughout Europe and the Middle East with twenty-five to thirty followers; when his fortunes fell, however, he found himself staying alone in a humble tavern or *bodegon* in Madrid (Subrahmanyan, 2011). The prominent Antwerp publisher, Christophe Plantin, was 'forever on the road' for a variety of reasons, but seems rarely to have travelled alone. Plantin journeyed regularly to the Frankfurt book fair with his right-hand man and future son-in-law Jan Moretus, while his wife and children accompanied him on some of his frequent trips to

Paris for business or personal motives (Imhof, 2020). The most eminent travellers moved with vast retinues, such as the ten thousand or so soldiers, servants, and nobles who escorted the Holy Roman Emperor Charles V when he sojourned briefly in Siena in 1536, en route from North Africa to Germany (Brizio, 2021; cf. also Guerzoni, 2010). At the other end of the scale, pedlars tended to travel in small companies, while pilgrims' accounts detail the ad hoc travelling partners often picked up on the road, even if one initially set out alone. Casual relationships were struck up and temporary companions acquired in confined spaces such as inns, boats, or coaches.

As this Element seeks to emphasize, many kinds of people, and many kinds of bodies, crowded the roads and waterways in this era, beyond the stereotypical (elite, male) Renaissance traveller. Men were certainly more likely to move, especially over long distances. However, the greatest number of them hailed from more humble social groups and professions, such as soldiers, sailors, craftsmen, or peasants transporting their produce. Mobility carried different connotations for female travellers, in a period when there could be much suspicion and disapproval of women who wandered about or ventured too far from their homes. As a result, and due to the dangers and hardships of travel, fewer women undertook long journeys in this era, and those who did were more likely to move with male relatives or chaperones or because they had little choice but to do so: as slaves or to flee from violence or persecution. Throughout the Middle Ages some female pilgrims had travelled as far as Rome, Santiago di Compostela, or even Jerusalem, but these 'wandering women' were often castigated for 'violat[ing] the spatial boundaries that defined behavior appropriate to their gender' (Craig, 2009: 23). From the seventeenth century, as crossing the continent became faster and easier, more and more women were able to travel for pilgrimage or pleasure, although still less often on lengthy 'Grand Tours' and more commonly to nearby capital cities or in their local areas (Sweet, 2012; Verhoeven, 2019; Akhimie & Andrea, 2019).

Moreover, throughout the Renaissance many women migrated for work, including the streams of women and girls, some as young as ten, who travelled from the countryside to cities to seek employment in domestic service or to start apprenticeships in professions such as the clothing trades (Bellavitis, 2006; see also Chojnacka, 2001). Some women also relocated later in life, such as the numerous widows who moved to Rome from other parts of Italy or Europe to find work as retailers, artisans, servants or in the hospitality sector after the death of their husbands (Canepari, 2013). Younger female migrants were seen as particularly vulnerable, even if they often relied on family members and compatriots to aid their journeys and their integration in a new place. The city of Venice, for example, introduced laws to try to prevent young girls who came to the metropolis to work as servants being lured into prostitution instead, mandating that they should stay only with respectable matrons in dedicated lodging houses until they found employment (Ferraro, 2016).[17]

Ultimately, mobility could both reinforce and challenge traditional gender stereotypes. Narratives of danger and adventure might serve to bolster elite masculine identities (especially when contrasted to supposedly fearful female or lower-class male travelling companions) (Verhoeven, 2019). But for many the act of moving meant stepping out of traditional roles and obligations, as in the case of the women who left their children behind to migrate in search of work or that of male migrants who lived in communal bachelor housing to support a family back at home (Canepari, 2014; Hamadeh, 2017). For both women and men, mobility could be a chance to leave behind a difficult family situation and embrace a new identity, as in the case of female renegades like the Venetian Beatrice Michiel, who abandoned her husband and children and moved to Constantinople in the late sixteenth century to be with a brother who worked in the Ottoman court, converting to Islam and taking the name Fatima Hatun (Dursteler, 2011). But such moves could render women, as well as men, extremely vulnerable, stranded between different worlds. This was demonstrated by the life story of Mariana di Fiori, a Jewish woman who migrated from her home in Danzig to Lebanon as a teenager around 1600; was captured by pirates while crossing the Mediterranean to Venice; was enslaved and (forcibly?) converted to Christianity; was impregnated by her noble Maltese owner; and then was sold on to another in Sicily. Once she was freed, Mariana moved with her young son to Italy and remarried a Christian, but he then denounced her to the Roman Inquisition for returning to her original Jewish faith (Siebenhühner, 2008).[18]

Travel was generally considered a dangerous enterprise in this period and not only for women. It was recognized as entailing significant physical and emotional trials and thus was thought to be better done by the young and sturdy. Gathering places such as crowded inns and lodging houses were particularly suspect as places of disease transmission. Regimens for those setting out on a trip counselled how a traveller might protect their body from physical threats and discomforts, ranging from seasickness (for which the advice was to drink seawater before departing, mixed with wine if one could afford it) to parasites to contracting syphilis from public baths or inn bedsheets (Horden, 2008). Still, extreme need could spur even the old or infirm out on long journeys, as in the

---

[17] On the mobility of working women on a smaller scale, see also Mansell (2021).

[18] For similar stories of women's mobility, captivity, and conversion in Renaissance theatre, see Jaffe-Berg (2016: chap. 3). On the figure of the convert, see also Das et al. (2021: 70–9).

case of patients who might travel long distances on foot to consult a medical practitioner or visit a hospital (Schmitz, 2023).[19]

Likewise, we also find cases of very young travellers braving the risks of the road. When his father died in 1526, the future Duke Cosimo I de' Medici, for instance, was sent away from Florence for safety. Aged only seven, Cosimo, accompanied by his tutor, servants, and some family members, set out on foot by night; convinced he was being abducted, he initially screamed and resisted desperately. Carrying on, the group faced numerous dangers as they tried to cross the peninsula in the midst of the Italian Wars. They eventually found their way safely to Venice, alternating transport by boat or horse with foot travel, although on at least one occasion Cosimo and his young cousins were so tired they had to be carried on the backs of their adult companions (Cappa, 2022: chap. 2).

Even for those who set off with healthy bodies, the rigours and risks of travel made it not unusual for them to fall ill on the road, sometimes forcing local contacts such as inn or lodging-house keepers to seek medical help. If treatment was unsuccessful, these same intermediaries might be called on to organize the dispersal of a deceased traveller's belongings post-mortem or, indeed, the transportation of the corpse back home. Presaging this possibility, some travellers, including many pilgrims, drew up wills before departing, including detailed clauses about what was to be done with their bodies and belongings if they died en route.

Aside from the risk of disease and accident, the bodies of Renaissance travellers were also seen to face considerable peril as a result of their exposure to different climates and especially to foreign foods (Earle, 2017). Moving to new places often meant being tempted – or forced – to taste unfamiliar dishes, whether local specialities or exotic offerings. While some embraced culinary novelties (and even tried to import them to their home regions), others saw eating foreign foods as a displeasure or even a danger and sought to avoid it. For example, William Biddulph, the chaplain sent to Aleppo by the East India Company in the early seventeenth century, refused the food offered by his Muslim hosts and instead insisted on having his meals cooked by his own servants as a way to 'hold on to his Protestant and English identity' (Ebrahim, 2021: 365).

Other travellers brought their own provisions. Such was the case, as we shall see further below, with many pilgrims who faced the uncertain quality and quantity of rations on vessels crossing to the Holy Land, as with the Spanish

---

[19] On the many peasants who travelled in from surrounding regions expressly to receive medical treatment in large urban hospitals, see Henderson (2006).

settlers who transported foodstuffs such as red wine, olive oil, and wheat to cultivate in the Americas so that their bodies would not have to adjust to a local diet. Slave traders might also supply enslaved Africans with familiar foods such as plantains, rice, yams, and couscous, in a bid to stop them falling victim to homesickness (Earle, 2017). Resistance to foreign foods could be motivated by religious reasons as much as health concerns, as with Jewish merchants who brought kosher food with them on ships crossing the Mediterranean and prepared it themselves (Arbel, 2017). Elsewhere, travellers were able to find safe places to eat with compatriots or at designated inns, as the Jewish goldsmith Salomone da Sesso discovered when he travelled from Bologna to Ferrara to work in the late fifteenth century and stayed at the local Jewish *osteria* (Herzig, 2019: 28–9).

Matters such as food, hygiene, and devotional practices were strongly tied to a person's sense of home. As a result, movement could be a profound and challenging emotional experience, surely even more so then than it is today (Boccagni & Baldassar, 2015). The sensory onslaught that might confront a new arrival to a foreign place could be deeply disorienting, especially when unknown languages were spoken, sounds and smells were different, and even matters as fundamental as time and distance were measured in unfamiliar ways. Homesickness was a common experience, although those who were literate (and could afford to send a letter) increasingly might mitigate it by correspondence with home, thanks to the expansion of commercial post services in this period (Matt, 2011; Verhoeven, 2023). Letters, sometimes sent along with 'care packages' of food, clothing, or money, could be potent emotional messengers connecting members of families separated by migration or exile (Broomhall, 2019; Dalton, 2020).

Loneliness also assailed travellers, especially when they were separated from companions. The Venetian pilgrim Bartolomeo Fontana, after parting ways with one temporary travel partner, resolved to continue from then onward on his own, claiming he could not bear the pain of losing another beloved comrade (Fontana, 1995: 21). Another pilgrim, Felix Fabri, was so overcome by fear when he set out from his home in Ulm on the long journey to the Holy Land that he had to overcome the desperate desire to turn back. The anxiety remained for his entire journey, leading Fabri to claim that he did not enjoy the experience, even if he did manage to accomplish his spiritual mission of pilgrimage (Fabri, 1896: 7).

2.2 Carrying Things

Studying what people elected to pack or acquire on the road can illuminate practices and expectations of mobility in penetrating ways. The emotional and physical trials associated with Renaissance mobility could be alleviated somewhat depending on what a person was able to take with them on their journeys. How much one could carry obviously depended greatly on means of transport and the circumstances under which one departed. European pilgrims crossing to the Holy Land, for example, were given only a small space each for personal baggage on board (Toffolo, 2018). On the other hand, the shift towards coach travel from the later sixteenth century allowed elite travellers over land to bring more luggage than had been possible on horse or mule transport (Verhoeven, 2023). Some people were obliged to leave in haste, taking almost nothing with them, such as some of the Jewish refugees who fled persecution in sixteenth-century Portugal. Others made room at least for objects that promised a protective function or allowed them to maintain their religious devotions on the road, like a wearable talisman or a portable altar (Mazzei, 2013: 13–16, 46, 170). At the other end of the scale, large entourages, such as those accompanying the Ottoman envoys who made their way to Venice, might move with an sizeable amount of luggage, including gifts such as carpets and luxury fabrics designed to impress their hosts (Pedani, 1994).

The many migrants who travelled to work took with them the tools and accoutrements of their trades. Such apparently prosaic items of luggage nonetheless must have been vitally important for the transmission of ideas, technologies, techniques, and practices across the continent (Cipolla, 1972; Ciriacono, 2005; Hilaire-Pérez & Verna, 2006). The first printers from northern Europe hauled their newly invented printing presses and metal typefaces across the Alps into Italy, where the art boomed and the necessary equipment then began to be produced locally (Santoro & Segatori, 2013). Medical charlatans transported their remedies and recipes, plus patents and licences from various authorities to display to the crowds who gathered to see them in markets, streets, and squares (Gentilcore, 2006), as depicted in a mid-seventeenth-century engraving by the Bolognese artist Giuseppe Maria Mitelli (Figure 7). Musicians carried their instruments. In his published deathbed lament, for instance, the itinerant singer and publisher of pamphlets Ippolito Ferrarese bid a tearful farewell to his beloved lyre which had accompanied him on his peregrinations all over the Italian peninsula in search of new audiences (Petrella, 2013). Professional beggars might transport images of saints which, at least according to the sixteenth-century *Book of Vagabonds*, they 'hang around their necks while they travel or move around cities, handing them to the faithful to kiss, placing them in front of church doors and in the streets so that passersby throw them some money' (Camporesi, 2007: 132). Messengers carried their decrees and missives in special cases emblazoned with the arms of the authorities who sent them on the road, such as one surviving example from Renaissance Bologna (Figure 8), while postal couriers' mailbags, with their precious cargoes of letters

Figure 7 Giuseppe Maria Mitelli, engraving of a charlatan mounted on a bench displaying his remedies and patents, mid seventeenth century. The Wellcome Collection. Attribution 4.0 International (CC BY 4.0).

and parcels, were frequent targets of theft, as depicted in Ferrante Pallavicino's satirical novel *Il corriere svaligiato* (1641) (Midura, 2019).

The nature and purpose of a journey also dictated what one could carry and how. For example, in 1572 a Cypriot spy sent to Constantinople to carry classified letters to the Venetian consul hid the correspondence in a waterproof piece of cloth which was then stitched up in a secret compartment in his clothes. Another spy working for the Venetians journeyed to the Ottoman capital with his own code book and instructions for the use of invisible ink (Iordannou, 2019: 183–5).

If someone could not travel personally they might transmit precious objects by proxy. The Brussels-born physician Andreas Vesalius, for instance, took pains to send the large and magnificent woodcut illustrations for his anatomical

Figure 8 Document case and lid inscribed with the arms of the Bentivoglio lords of Bologna, used to transport official documents, ca. 1475–1525. Victoria and Albert Museum, London.

textbook *De humani corporis fabrica* from Padua, where he taught at the University, to the book's printer in Basel by means of some Milanese merchants, along with a detailed letter describing exactly how to compose the text and images. But Vesalius also noted that he would 'strive to journey to you soon, and I shall remain in Basel, if not for the whole period of printing, at least for some time', so that he could personally oversee the production of his masterpiece (Vesalius, 1950: 46–7). The Venetian artist Lorenzo Lotto, meanwhile, meticulously recorded his expenditure on ropes, bars, nails, and canvas coverings to protect his paintings as well as the costs of having them transported safely by land and sea to patrons elsewhere in Italy (Lotto, 2017). More prosaically, in early modern Spain, if a sick person could not travel themselves, samples of their hair or urine might be transported to a reputed doctor or healer far away, sometimes by means of dedicated 'piss messengers' (Schmitz, 2023).

Some travellers passed advice along in person about the necessary items to bring with them, as well as writing it down in their accounts or guidebooks destined to be read by other would-be voyagers. Pilgrims passing through Venice on their way to the east, for instance, were advised to stock up on food and other useful items for their journeys. The Dutchman Arendt Willemsz suggested buying red wine, fresh water, dry bread, sausages, cheese, butter, sugar, and olive oil, among other things, on the assumption that the provisions on board the ship would not be sufficient. The Frenchman Jacques le Saige added candles, towels, and mousetraps to his list. Other pilgrims noted how necessities such as bedding and mattresses might be purchased in Venice before embarking for the east and sold again there on the way home thanks to the city's flourishing second-hand market, allowing them to recoup around half of the costs. Venice's booming publishing industry also provided another desirable commodity for pilgrims: printed books, including guides to holy places which might be carried attached to belts or saddles; many also stocked up on paper and ink to be able to write their own accounts on the way (Toffolo, 2018; Bale & Beebe, 2021).

Post-mortem inventories can give us another window into what people took with them when they moved. When the Turkish merchant Hüyseīn Çelebī was murdered in Venice in 1575, for example, an inventory of his belongings was made so that they could be sold there. These included items to alleviate the challenges of the lengthy trip (likely overland from Anatolia to the Dalmatian coast and then by boat across the Adriatic) such as warm clothes for winter travel, sturdy covers for horses, and wax-cloth for protecting the merchandise he brought from the Ottoman Empire to trade, probably goods such as silk, camlets, carpets, and leather. But there were also items offering alternative kinds of protection (some written prayers and weapons) and objects that may have helped to recreate some of the customs of home, including cooking utensils, a coffee or teacup, a ewer that may have served as a kettle, and opiates kept in a small box or hookah (Kafadar, 1986: 212–16).

Heading in the other direction, some inventories survive of Italian merchants and others who died in Damascus in the fifteenth century. These documents again suggest the sorts of practical, everyday items that such temporary migrants might acquire to assist their work in a new place (office equipment, material for packing merchandise) or to pass the time on long voyages (such as the copies of St Jerome's *Lives of the Saints* and Boccaccio's *Elegy of Madonna Fiammetta* that the merchant Nicolò de Ruzino da Feltre carried with him on board the galley heading to Beirut on which he died). The post-mortem inventory of a Venetian oarsman who died at his bench on the Beirut galley reveals the meagre possessions of a much more modest kind of migrant: Andrea da Raguxio had little more than a small amount of goods to sell, some money, and a broken cutlass, although he also left two barrels of wine to his fellow rowers. These inventories similarly suggest the kinds of novel foreign items that could be acquired locally while residing abroad, from a 'Moorish' copper cooking pot and musical instruments to carpets and Damascene metalwork and paper (Bianchi & Howard, 2003).

Exposure to unfamiliar forms of material culture while on the move led to the transmission of patterns, techniques, and styles. We witness this also in the case of artists. Vasari's life of the engraver Marcantonio Raimondi, for example, recounts how, 'seized, as happens to many, with a desire to go about the world and see new things and the methods of other craftsmen', Raimondi travelled from Bologna to Venice in the early sixteenth century. 'About the same time,' Vasari continues, 'there arrived in Venice some Flemings with many copper-plate engravings and woodcuts by [the Nuremberg artist] Albrecht Dürer, which were seen by Marc'Antonio on the Piazza di S. Marco.' Raimondi, 'so amazed at the manner and method of the work of Albrecht . . . spent on those sheets almost all the money that he had brought from Bologna', an acquisition that would have a major influence on Raimondi's practice and career, as he then produced copies of the northern artist's *Life of the Virgin* series. Vasari also claims that this episode provoked Dürer's second visit to Italy shortly after, in order to defend his intellectual property in the Venetian courts (Vasari, 1912–15: VI, 95–6). Although the precise truth of this story is now questioned, there is no doubt that the Nuremberg artist was likewise profoundly influenced by his own encounters with the artistic and material culture of the lagoon city. As well as interacting with local artists and patrons, Dürer's letters attest that in Venice he enthusiastically acquired printed books, paper, jewels, carpets, glass, feathers, and rosary beads both for himself and his patron Willibald Pirckheimer (Di Lenardo, 2018).

When they had the chance to travel, women could also be enthusiastic consumers of foreign goods, as the case of Dürer's own wife Agnes demonstrates. While she did not come to Venice, Agnes accompanied her husband to Flanders and the Low Countries in 1520–1. In Antwerp she acquired goods including cooking utensils, stockings, and shoes for herself, as well as a cage for a parrot (imported from the New World and given as a gift to her husband) (Mazzei, 2013: 63). Even women who did not travel far themselves might also participate in the circulation of material goods and encounter foreign novelties. As Bianchi and Howard note, for example, 'as recipients of bequests [from their male relatives in the Levant], women at home in Venice were important conduits for the channelling of eastern material culture into Venetian daily life' (2003: 240).

Along with commodities and souvenirs, from the sixteenth century various kinds of travel guidebooks became an increasingly common feature in the luggage of people on the move. Even as most practical information about travel still passed by word of mouth or letters between friends, colleagues, and family members, printed guides proliferated with the rise of print culture and offered a good deal of useful assistance to travellers. Guides to the road systems (the first printed one being Charles Estienne's *Le guide des chemins de France*, 1552) informed about different routes and the distances between locations; guides to the postal network (starting with the *Nuovo itinerario delle poste per tutto il mondo* by Ottavio Codogno, the deputy postmaster general of the state of Milan, in 1608) described the crucial nodes in this expanding system of transport, communication, and hospitality (Maczak, 1995: 24; Midura, 2019). Printed phrase books multiplied and give us insight into some of the key concerns and interests of travellers. One for Italian merchants and travellers to the Levant provides Turkish phrases for everything from conducting a business deal to asking a woman for sexual favours (Palumbo-Fossati, 2006: 341). Such information was available not just for the most elite travellers. The English poet and Thames waterman John Taylor used his personal, extensive experience of mobility to write several cheap guides, such as *The Carriers Cosmography: or A Brief Relation of The Innes, Ordinaries, Hostelries, and other lodgings in, and near London . . .* (1637) (Capp, 1994: chap. 1) (Figure 9).

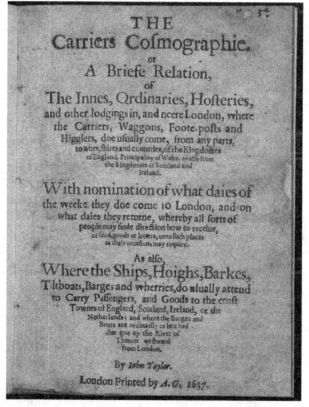

Figure 9 Title page of John Taylor's *The Carriers Cosmographie . . .* (London: A[nne] G[riffin], 1637). Call no. 13692. The Huntington Library, San Marino, California.

Guidebooks and maps also increasingly allowed people to travel virtually, without facing the physical risks of moving. Already in the fourteenth century, the poet Petrarch – who in fact roamed widely across Europe – declared his decision

> not to travel just once on a very long journey by ship or horse or on foot . . . but many times on a tiny map, with books and the imagination, so that in the course of an hour I could go to those shores and return as many times as I liked . . . not only unscathed, but unwearied too, not only with sound body, but with no wear and tear to my shoes untouched by rains, stones, mud and dust. (quoted in Horodowich, 2018: 112)

This kind of 'armchair travel' was ever more possible as printed maps, costume books documenting the dress and customs of foreign peoples, and travel accounts became increasingly abundant and accessible from the sixteenth century (Wilson, 2005; Calvi, 2022).

Renaissance travellers who did set out on the road also were more and more likely to carry with them written or printed identification documents of various kinds – indeed, these might be among the most important items that they brought along. These documents were a fundamental part of the expanding infrastructure of surveillance and control of mobility considered in Section 1, as they progressively replaced earlier forms of marking the moving body with signs or symbols: from the badges of licensed beggars to the red wax coated on the thumbnail of people allowed to enter certain cities (Simeoni, 1934: 81; Groebner, 2007: chap. 2).[20] The publisher Plantin, for example, petitioned for royal safe conducts and passports (including permission to carry firearms) to be able to travel safely from Antwerp to France and back with his family and servants (Imhof, 2020). Highly mobile individuals and groups, from pedlars to the first acting troupes of the Commedia dell'arte, had to become especially proficient at negotiating with different bureaucratic systems to obtain the necessary licences and permits to move (Fietta Ielen, 1985: 56–7; Ferrone, 1993: 23).

Aside from documents issued by state or religious institutions, a more personal variety was the handwritten letter of recommendation or introduction from an eminent person, which might be sent ahead or carried by the traveller. These were particularly prevalent in professional or scholarly networks such as the emerging Republic of Letters or those of international merchants seeking to establish trust across distance (Trivellato, 2007; Aslanian, 2020). That they did not always have the desired effect is suggested by a drawing by Federico Zuccaro (Figure 10), which depicts his

---

[20] However, on the continuing use of yellow badges to identify Jewish travellers throughout the later sixteenth century, see Cassen (2019).

Figure 10 Drawing by Federico Zuccaro depicting his brother Taddeo as a young immigrant to Rome handing a letter of introduction to his cousin, the painter Francesco il Sant'Angelo, and being rebuffed, ca. 1595. Getty Collection.

brother Taddeo arriving as a young immigrant painter to Rome and being rebuffed by a kinsman of theirs, also a painter, despite proffering a letter of introduction (discussed also by Young Kim, 2014: 219–20). The classics professor Martin Crusius in Wolfenbüttel took particular interest in the letters of identification and presentation brought to him by his numerous Greek visitors (one carried as many as fourteen such letters), copying out the foreign seals and signatures that they bore on them as signs of their authenticity (Calis, 2019).

2.3 Dress and Dissembling

As this last example implies, the multiplication of travel documents also fed a market for fakes, so that individuals had to work hard to discern authentic ones and authorities had to keep each other up to date so that they could each be on the lookout for forgeries (Bamji, 2019; Eliav-Feldon, 2012). In the last part of this section, I want to consider briefly how Renaissance mobility could also be an occasion for disguising one's body and identity in various ways, a practice in which fake documents might figure prominently.

Given the physical challenges of mobility discussed already, it is not surprising that people setting out on a journey gave a lot of thought to, and advised other travellers about, the important choice of which clothes to wear on the road. Hats (straw in summer and felt in winter), cloaks, and sturdy shoes were particularly crucial, as frontline protection against the elements, especially if travelling on foot, horse, or mule (Maczak, 1995: 105; Riello, 2010). The wrong clothes could be a major hindrance, as the artist Cellini became painfully aware when he tried to climb a mountain in the Alps 'completely clothed in mail, with big boots, and a gun in my hand; and it was raining as though the fountains of the heavens were opened' (1995: 180).

But changing place could also mean changing clothes, even if, as with food, this could be a matter of either choice or compulsion. Some travellers preferred to adopt the dress of the places they moved to and even retain it when they came home as a 'visible and public way of proclaiming cosmopolitan identities' (Gallagher, 2017: 104–5).[21] Altering appearance could be a sign of the profound personal transformations that moving both engendered and expressed, as in the case of escaped slaves or servants who communicated their reconversion to Islam by reverting to eastern-style clothes or shaving their heads (Burke, 2013; cf. Ebrahim, 2021).

---

[21] On the increasing global circulation of information about and images of clothing from different parts of the world in this period, see Calvi (2022).

Many others, however, opted to change clothes (as well as comportment, language, or accent) to blend in or to conceal their identity. Venetian merchants trading in the Levant, for example, were granted the privilege of being able to dress *a la morescha* (in the Moorish style), for their own security (Bianchi & Howard, 2003: 247). The Jesuit Matteo Ricci, meanwhile, chose to garb himself as a Confucian scholar when conducting missionary work in China so as to 'translate' his social position to the locals (Burke, 2007: 9). A more dramatic example is provided again by Cellini, who recounts in his *Vita* how he disguised himself as a friar to flee Florence when he was wanted for murder; once outside the city he was able to remove his monk's habit, mount a horse, and escape by night to Siena (1995: 27). In contrast, the reformist cleric Bernardino Ochino was compelled to dress in the clothes of a layperson when fleeing the clutches of the Italian Inquisition across the Alps in the 1540s (Mazzei, 2013: 155).

Adopting a different appearance could be an essential form of protection against the dangers of moving in foreign lands. As the aforementioned examples from Fynes Moryson's *Itinerary* imply, in an age of increasing confessional division new dangers confronted travellers, who might be forced to disguise themselves for safety. Indeed, Moryson's general advice was that 'a traveller must sometimes hide his money, change his habit, dissemble his Country, and fairely conceale his Religion', although he added that 'this hee must doe onely when necessity forceth' (1617: II, 30). Eating and drinking habits could also be an important marker of identity that might need to be concealed on the road. Other Northern Europeans in Italy in the Reformation era feared that ordering meat dishes on 'lean' days would identify them as Lutherans and lead to trouble (Zaniboni, 1921: 40; see also Mazzei, 2013: 134–5).

And yet, changing place might also provide more liberating opportunities to not just disguise oneself temporarily but to adopt wholly new identities, even crossing boundaries of class, gender, or faith. The further one travelled from home, the more these kinds of transformations were possible. As Eliav-Feldon writes, 'the opening of geographical horizons and the fantastic news reaching Europe from across the world created another early modern setting for the invention of identities. By escaping to one of the "new worlds", far away from the watchful eyes of family, neighbours and friends, to places where church and state controls were at least more lax than at home if not non-existent, women could join the army as male soldiers, conversos and their offspring could more easily pass for scions of Old Christian families, and commoners could pass for nobles' (2012: 10). A case in point is that of Thomas, or Thomasine, Hall, who dressed alternatively as a man or a woman as he/she migrated from their birthplace in Newcastle-upon-Tyne to London, then to France as a soldier, then back to Plymouth, and finally to colonial Virginia as a servant in the early seventeenth century (Canny, 1994: 263–4).

With so many people on the move in different directions, however, there was heightened suspicion of fakes and disguises. Much of this was targeted at the ever more numerous mobile poor, who – according to popular catalogues of 'false beggars' and vagabonds – might dress up as friars, pilgrims, or priests or even contort their bodies to feign disabilities and diseases to elicit charity (Camporesi, 2007). There was also growing fascination with spies, another particularly mobile group emerging in this period who adopted multiple alternative kinds of dress and appearance (as fishermen, pilgrims, merchants, peasants, and many others) to conceal their real identities on the move (Iordannou, 2019). It is no wonder, then, that the Renaissance has been described as an 'age of imposters', when Europeans 'suffered from an obsession concerning identification and from a deep anxiety that things were not what they seemed and people were not who they said they were' (Eliav-Feldon, 2012: 3).

If there was increasing apprehension about how to identify and authenticate people in this period, then it was closely related to escalating and accelerating mobility, which undermined traditional relationships of trust upon which identity and reputation were built (Buono, 2015). Recently scholars have pointed to a broader early modern 'crisis of recognizability' that, according to Aslanian, 'was itself a symptom in part of a larger crisis of vagrancy and mobility' (2019: 137; see also Groebner, 2007; Ghobrial, 2019). As described here and in the previous section, Renaissance authorities devised new ways to mark out and identify the bodies of people on the move, to make visible who did and did not belong, who had the right to move and who did not. We have also seen how more and more use was made of forms of paper documentation, which went hand in hand with bureaucratic record-keeping practices to allow civic, and increasingly also state, authorities to have a better sense of who was entering or passing through their territory.

At the same time, travellers and migrants actively assessed the risks and opportunities that mobility afforded and sought to prepare themselves physically and mentally for the experience. It is evident that moving – even over relatively short distances, but even more so over longer ones – could have a profound impact on people's bodies and intimate habits: on how one ate, where (and with whom) one slept, how one dressed, and how one performed religious rituals. Encounters with foreign landscapes, climates, people, and objects similarly left their mark. And all of these things might fundamentally affect a person's sense of themselves and of others, their view of where they came from and of the world, in some cases making them feel even more of a stranger if and when they did return 'home' (Subrahmanyam, 2011: 179).

3 Agents of Exchange

In the backstreets behind Venice's main port area in the 1580s, Paolina Briani was one of many local women who made their living renting out rooms to foreigners. The majority of Paolina's tenants were Greek and Ottoman Muslim merchants who came to trade in the great entrepôt city. It is only thanks to a trial of the Venetian Inquisition that we know something of Paolina's activities. Although it is difficult to ascertain if the allegations that she allowed 'many enormous sins and wickedness' to go on under her roof were true, the trial – including Paolina's own testimony and those of her neighbours, friends, and tenants – testifies to her activity as a broker on multiple fronts: economic, sexual, cultural, and even culinary.[22]

Witnesses declared that the unmarried Paolina, who was likely also a prostitute, had sexual relations with her Muslim guests, even bearing a child to one, and that she procured Christian prostitutes for the men in her house. It was claimed that she invited over local Greek women and girls from the neighbourhood to tell fortunes and to pursue other pastimes that the Inquisition considered superstitious or irreligious. Moreover, Paolina was accused of turning a blind eye to promiscuous religious practices among her tenants, particularly in the case of a Christian Armenian servant, Gregorio, working for a Turkish merchant who was staying in the house. The merchant, Hussain of Tocat, allegedly forced his young employee to dress like a Muslim and to follow Muslim customs, including eating meat on days prohibited to Christians. In her own defence, Paolina claimed that she simply allowed her multi-ethnic lodgers to follow their own religious rites, especially in relation to food: the 'Greeks follow Greek customs, and the Turks, Turkish ones, so that the Turks eat meat on Friday and the Greeks on Saturday'.

The investigation, which the Inquisition eventually dropped for unknown reasons, provides a window into what was just one of many such houses, in Venice and other Renaissance cities, where ordinary women and men made their living as providers of hospitality and thus also as brokers of mobility and cultural exchange. Paolina herself was a local and stayed in the same parish for at least another twenty years. Her case thus also reminds us that 'intermediation is not synonymous with peregrination' (Raj, 2016: p. 51); many Renaissance go-betweens were not highly mobile themselves, even if a good number might draw on their own past experiences of migration, or their ability to navigate and translate between cultures and languages, to act as vital brokers between different people, places, and traditions.

---

[22] Archivio di stato, Venice, Sant'Uffizio, busta 47, fasc. 2. See the discussion of this case and of other lodging-house keepers in Salzberg (2019).

Cases like Paolina's complement and nuance research since the 1990s that has highlighted the role of some highly mobile individuals or intermediaries who crossed both physical and cultural borders with seeming ease, usually more elite or educated men who left written records of their travels (e.g. Greenblatt, 1991; Zemon Davis, 2006; Burke & Hsia, 2007).[23] This kind of 'going between' has been described as 'a major driving force of Renaissance culture . . . fuel[ing] the unprecedented circulation of political, social, religious and artistic ideas which permeates and indeed defines this period' (Höfele & Von Koppenfels, 2005: 4). In this section I want to highlight the work of a variety of more ordinary agents of mobility and exchange who have emerged in recent research. Some of these figures were indeed professionally mobile, like pedlars and itinerant performers. Some, such as a good number of translators and interpreters, used their personal familiarity with migration and travel to aid their work as multilingual cultural mediators. Others, such as innkeepers, lodging-house keepers like Paolina Briani, and postmasters, may have been more settled and integrated into local communities but still did vital work in enabling different kinds of interaction with and between mobile people. Such individuals were not exceptional but in fact ever-present in Renaissance life, in large cities but also on the roads and in rural areas. A closer look at them can help us to better understand both the bridges and the boundaries to the intercultural interaction that energized the Renaissance: the intense connection between mobility and cultural exchange but also the 'friction and discomfort' that habitual border crossers encountered (Subrahmanyam, 2011: 175).

3.1 Pedlars and Itinerant Performers

Much has been written about the role of merchants as the trailblazers of Medieval and Renaissance mobility, often the first to tread paths then followed by other mobile individuals from diplomats to labourers (e.g. Cowan, 2000). Despite being in many cases only temporary migrants – staying for a few weeks, months, or years in another place, albeit perhaps returning multiple times – merchants engaged in numerous kinds of exchanges with the communities they visited, beyond the transaction of goods and money: the transfer of everything from news and ideas to recipes, pastimes, and vocabulary (Kafadar, 1986). Armenian merchants, for instance, trading across an increasingly global maritime diaspora from the fifteenth century on, were instrumental in the promotion of early print culture, by making financing and transport infrastructure available to publishers based in port cities (Aslanian, 2014). The agency of merchants as both cultural and commercial brokers was facilitated by their interactions with

---

[23] More recently, see Das (2022).

a great variety of individuals in foreign ports and markets as well as en route: from local customs officials to interpreters, commercial brokers, and petty retailers (Harreld, 2003). Nor should we forget the army of transport workers who followed in the wake of merchants or were essential to the conduct of trade in local contexts: from packers and porters to carters and mule-drivers.

Indeed, once we look beyond the high-level merchants who coordinated large-scale, transnational operations, we can see that the roads of Renaissance Europe and the streets of its cities were increasingly crowded with more modest, mobile commercial operators. Pedlars played a critical but often overlooked part in bringing both everyday staple items and low-level luxury goods to urban and rural dwellers (Fontaine, 1996; Van den Heuvel, 2012). The cries of itinerant vendors – and the sights and smells of their merchandise – were ubiquitous in Renaissance cities. Images of them that began to proliferate from the late sixteenth century (such as seen in Figure 11) show them selling everything from food (donuts, prawns, eggs, milk, and so on) to combs, books, fans, and soap, carried and displayed in baskets, on trays, hoisted on poles, or laden onto carts and the backs of horses or donkeys (Calaresu, 2020). If the Renaissance was marked by increasing consumerism, pedlars performed a critical part in this process by diffusing a great variety of goods beyond the restricted circles of urban elites. Meanwhile, longer-range pedlars helped to disseminate minor luxuries to smaller towns and rural areas, such as the chapmen who spread across England in the same period and enabled a 'minor revolution in domestic comfort' among the poor, by bringing them affordable goods such as linens and handkerchiefs (Spufford, 1984: 146).

While the itinerancy of many such traders means they tend to disappear from the historical record, occasionally documents survive which allow us to paint a more detailed picture of their presence and activity. Matriculation records for Florence's guild of doctors and spice-dealers from the late fifteenth century on, for example, record a very large number of more or less mobile outdoor vendors selling around the city and/or across the wider Florentine state. Notably, many of these were immigrants or itinerant traders from other parts of Italy or Europe. Examples include Giovanni Battista, a converted Jew from Ferrara listed as singing in the street and selling stories, soap, and rosaries (1540); Marco Antonio the German, who pulled teeth and sold powders and unguents (1546); and Giovanni di Lorenzo from Flanders, who peddled Flemish prints and paintings (1591).[24] Such examples suggest the importance of informal trading as a recourse for migrants trying to get by in a new place but also the

---

[24] Archivio di Stato, Florence, Arte dei medici e speziali, reg. 11, c. 131v; reg. 22, c. 141r; reg. 13, c. 278v. For more on these pedlars, see Salzberg (2020).

Figure 11 Detail from the etching *Portrait of those who go selling and working around Rome* (Ambrogio Brambilla, *Ritrato di qvelli che vanno vendendo e lavorando per Roma . . .*, Roma: Apresso Andrea Vaccario, 1612). Folger Shakespeare Library, Digital Image Collection, Call no. ART 231- 749 (size L) (CC BY-SA 4.0).

ways in which pedlars acted as vital transmitters of novel forms of material culture, trends, and styles across large distances.

After the invention of the press in the mid-fifteenth century, pedlars were especially crucial in the capillary dissemination of cheap printed texts and images, transporting them to ever greater audiences not just in the major urban centres but also in rural areas. At the same time, they also promoted the spread of a pan-European print culture marked by common themes, genres, and material forms (Harms, Raymond & Salman, 2013). This made them essential vectors of communication, spreading new and sometimes 'dangerous' ideas, as in the case of the two Frenchman found in Parma in 1558 in possession of around 600 copies of printed portraits of Martin Luther and other German reformers, which they admitted to having peddled around numerous other northern Italian cities (Ceriotti & Dallasta, 2009; cf. Griffin, 2007).

Research on pedlars has revealed that many of them were less marginal and isolated than we might assume, with some developing ever more sophisticated mobile commercial operations that linked rural and urban areas and later would also extend well beyond Europe to other parts of the world. A telling example is the pedlars from the Tesino valley in the Italian Dolomites, mountain-dwellers who adapted their seasonal migration patterns of transhumance into a new career as itinerant salesmen. At first peddling the excellent local flint used in firearms, from the seventeenth century the Tesini began to collaborate with the flourishing printing industry in the nearby town of Bassano, eventually forming what was probably the largest network of print distributors in Europe, spreading from Spain to Russia. From the Remondini press in particular they sold a range of cheap pamphlets, images, and objects of both religious and profane natures (from pictures of saints or the crucifixion, used for personal devotion and contemplation, to game boards and calendars). These 'rustic' mountain-dwellers managed to learn the languages of the places to which they travelled, negotiate with local authorities to obtain licences and health passes that facilitated their mobility, and transmit crucial information about customer preferences back to the urban producers of the goods they peddled (Fietta Ielen, 1985; Salzberg, 2020). At the same time, in another example of how mobility and immobility could be intrinsically entwined, the seasonal selling trips of small groups of Tesino men were supported and enabled by the hard work of their wives, mothers, sisters, and daughters who stayed behind in the valley and even invested their dowries in their family peddling enterprises (Caramel, 2019).

Sharing the roads with pedlars were growing numbers of itinerant performers who made their way through Renaissance towns and cities, playing or singing from temporary benches and stages at strategic sites such as marketplaces, squares, and bridges like Paris' Pont-Neuf or Venice's Rialto. Itinerant singers and musicians had been circulating for centuries, their repertoires covering an extraordinary range of genres, from chivalric epics to political commentary and news, from bawdy love poems to religious songs. The Renaissance saw them emerge as increasingly defined and professional figures, allying their performances to the sale of consumer goods such as medicines, soaps, and printed pamphlets and sometimes of works they had composed and/or published themselves (Salzberg & Rospocher, 2012). Quick to spy the communicative potential of the new technology of printing from the late fifteenth century, street performers became especially important transmitters of news in this period, rapidly recounting every major story in song and cheap print, from the latest bloody battle in the Italian Wars to the assassination of a leader or the execution of a heretic or criminal (McIlvenna, 2016; Hyde, 2018). As such, they could be critical in shaping public opinion and a sense of common identity, whether by spreading dissenting ideas or singing their support for the status quo (Degl'Innocenti & Rospocher, 2019a). The incessant mobility of such figures who could not sustain their careers in one place was crucial to their capacity to disseminate texts and ideas and to reach diverse publics. According to McShane, for example, English ballad singers 'brought the popular musical productions of the metropolis to the provinces (though this was not entirely a one-way process), acting as cultural mediators between town and country, centre and periphery, orality and print' (2019: 95).[25]

While the often humble and highly mobile nature of these figures makes it very difficult to trace individual biographies, we know of a few prominent examples, usually thanks to their ongoing involvement with the press. The street singer and charlatan Jacopo Coppa, for example, left his native Modena and was active in cities all over Italy in the sixteenth century, from Venice to Naples. As well as working as a healer and pedlar of medical remedies in the piazza, Coppa's career 'traverses the peaks of Renaissance literary culture', as he also performed and published new works by leading contemporary writers like Pietro Aretino and Lodovico Ariosto, as well as his own classically inspired poetry (Degl'Innocenti & Rospocher, 2019b: 21). Indeed, Aretino, who witnessed Coppa reciting his poems from a bench on the piazza in Ferrara, claimed to be delighted to hear his words 'in the mouths of charlatans', as this was the most effective way to reach a large and diverse public at this time (Salzberg, 2010).

At the same time, it was precisely the itinerance of individuals like Coppa that tended to arouse suspicion. The Modenese performer, for his part, continually came into conflict with local medical boards who were alarmed by his

---

[25] Cf. also Brayshay (2005); Zur Nieden & Over (2016).

unorthodox healing practices, while he also fell under suspicion of blasphemy and Protestant heresy that led to interrogation by secular and ecclesiastical magistracies and, on one occasion, to his banishment from Venice. And Coppa was not alone: the mobility of many performers, as well as pedlars, frequently provoked hostility and occasionally led them to be expelled en masse along with other marginal figures. In England, for example, the 1572 poor law introduced harsh measures against all those identified as vagabonds, including pedlars, minstrels, and actors (Henke, 2015: 33; Hitchcock, 2020). Because of their mobility and frequenting of places of gathering such as inns, itinerant professionals also were commonly linked to the spread of disease and could be denied licences to travel or to perform when plague was rife (Brayshay, 2005: 434, 450). Pedlars in particular might be pursued and punished both by guilds and local traders wanting to rid themselves of competition and by police trying to clear the streets of what they regarded as noise and nuisance (Van den Heuvel, 2015).

In some places, itinerant traders and performers found ways to gain some degree of acceptance and legitimation. One was to form or join guilds or confraternities that afforded them some access to mutual support and a collective voice. Blind singers in some Spanish cities, for instance, organized themselves into brotherhoods partly to distinguish themselves from lowly beggars, gaining thereby a monopoly to go around reciting prayers in return for money and later also to peddle cheap print (Gomis, 2019).

We see similar trends in Renaissance theatre, as actors also began to form more regular companies from the sixteenth century, with predictable timetables of movement that helped both to legitimize their mobility and to enhance their safety and reputation. Near-constant travel, across both regions and national borders, was essential to the economic success of many acting groups, as they needed to perform both for broad urban publics and for more elite audiences in courts or noble residences (Ferrone, 1993; Palmer, 2005). By the late sixteenth century, the English company of the Queen's Men, for example, travelled on average 'more than 1500 miles (2400 km) and performed in at least twenty-eight different places each year' (Brayshay, 2005: 448). It is perhaps no surprise, too, that the formation of the first Italian Commedia dell'arte troupe is dated to a contract of 1545 in which the actors collectively purchased a horse, likely used to carry their props and costumes from town to town as they themselves would have travelled on foot (Jaffe-Berg, 2016: 47).

Physical mobility was also integral to the cultural impact of the Italian Commedia, which has been described as 'from its very inception the perfect transnational machine' because of its 'language of gesture and acrobatic-style theater, [which] traveled well across regions and nations' (Henke, 1991: 19).

The movements of courts and nobles (for example, with the Florentine Marie de' Medici's marriage to the French King Henry IV in 1600) encouraged the journeys of Italian actors across Europe and, with them, the transmission of plots, scenarios, acting styles, and stock characters like the Zanni/Arlecchino. Italian merchants stationed in cities like Lyons and Antwerp provided another important source of support for these travelling performers. Renaissance actors also drew heavily on their own personal experiences of mobility when composing their plays, as well as reflecting the mobile and culturally diverse publics for which they performed. The actor and head of the Gelosi troupe, Francesco Andreini, for example, had served as a soldier for the Duke of Tuscany and been imprisoned by the Ottomans for eight years (Jaffe-Berg, 2016: 26). It comes as no surprise then that 'themes of travel, conversion, shifting identity and intercultural contact with Mediterranean peoples are abundantly present' in the scenarios of the Commedia, as is 'the paraphernalia of travel': props such as 'travelling clothes, lanterns for night travel, as well as exotic goods (carpets, medicines, potions)' (ibid.: 4, 66). If migration and mobility made actors and other performers suspicious to many people, as potential carriers of disease or dangerous ideas, it was also crucial to their exceptional power as cultural mediators, whether between different publics or across linguistic and political borders.

3.2 Translators and Interpreters

As the actors of the Commedia dell'arte knew, mobility over any significant distance also was likely to mean crossing linguistic boundaries. Many migrants and travellers managed this process themselves, using gestures or a common lingua franca or by learning enough of a foreign dialect or language to 'get by' even if they never reached fluency. Curiosity or necessity encouraged people to find ways to communicate across language barriers. The German pilgrim Felix Fabri, for instance, recounts having to resort to sign language at a hostelry in the Italian town of Bassano where no one spoke German, while in another inn near Ulm, in southern Germany, the Florentine ambassador Francesco Vettori found common ground discoursing in rough Latin with a local priest who was curious to learn about Italian life (Fabri, 1896: 10; Kümin & Tlusty, 2011: II, 294).

As Gallagher has shown, language learning was becoming another important motivation for mobility in this period, and travellers were 'urged to treat their environment as a pedagogical tool', immersing themselves in conversation with locals of every kind to improve their language skills, from nuns at convent gates to lodging-house keepers. Thomas Hoby, the translator of Castiglione's *Book of the Courtier*, purposefully chose to avoid other Englishmen when travelling in

Italy so that he could better learn the language, while his compatriot Fynes Moryson advised a similar approach (Gallagher, 2019: 170, 189). Those who were able to communicate directly by learning local languages could operate more safely and effectively in foreign contexts. Such was the case with the Italian Jesuit Matteo Ricci who, unlike many Europeans in China in this period, managed to master Chinese and thus became a crucial mediator with local authorities and in knowledge transmission via the translation of scientific texts (Bonnotte-Hoover, 2021).

Some parts of Renaissance Europe were particularly intense sites of multilingual exchange. Dursteler (2012) has noted, for example, how, in the Mediterranean area, the prevalence of slavery, labour migration, and war, as well as trade, travel, and diplomacy, encouraged both professional and practical multilingualism. Large multicultural cities (especially ports like Venice, Lisbon, or Antwerp) were especially distinguished by the babel of languages that could be heard there, making it easier for a new arrival to function in their native tongue but also favouring the adoption of new languages (Gschwend & Lowe, 2015). The French writer Montaigne similarly commented on how Rome was 'the most universal city in the world . . . you hardly see a beggar who does not ask alms of us in our own language' (2003: 1173–4). Border areas were also 'contact zones' (Pratt, 1992) where high levels of linguistic (and other kinds of) exchange took place: spaces where one transitioned from one language to another or found a mixture of languages and dialects. Travelling south through the Alps around 1580, Montaigne (again) remarked that 'about two leagues above [the northern Italian city of] Trent, the Italian language begins', as one passed out of German-speaking lands, although in fact the city had a sizeable German migrant community (2003: 1112).

While Montaigne himself learnt enough Italian to switch into this language while writing his travel diary, he also used an interpreter in various places, such as the town messenger whom he employed for this purpose in Basel (ibid.: 1073–4). Nor was he alone: pilgrims and other travellers often made use of guides or interpreters, both locals and multilingual foreigners, such as the Spanish renegade engaged by the German pilgrim Von Harff in the Holy Land (Arbel, 2017: 188). From the late Middle Ages, Venetian *tolomazi* or official guides were assigned to visiting pilgrims who did not have other contacts in the city and needed linguistic assistance, to help them find accommodation, contract passage on a galley, and obtain supplies for the trip to the east (Davis & Marvin, 2004: 24–5). In Rome, *ciceroni* offered their services to foreign visitors from the late sixteenth century (Zaniboni, 1921: 149).

More or less professional translators and interpreters undoubtedly were fundamental facilitators of diplomatic, religious, commercial, and literary exchanges across the Renaissance world (Burke, 2007; Tessicini, 2014). These kinds of multilingual mediators often were peripatetic or else had long histories of mobility before they settled down to work in one place. For example, many of the Ottoman Grand Dragomans or interpreters in the sixteenth century – figures like Yunus Bey, born Giorgio Taroniti in the Greek town of Methoni, a former Venetian colony – were converts to Islam and former captives 'whose familiarity with foreign languages, speech styles, and courtly etiquette was essential for their success' (Rothman, 2011: 167; see also Rothman, 2021). Such 'transimperial subjects' were vital conduits in the production and circulation of news in and from Constantinople, providing invaluable local knowledge and helping European diplomats – who usually did not speak Turkish – to navigate the Ottoman court. These skills could place interpreters in positions of considerable power and see them remunerated handsomely for their services: Yunus Bey left a fortune of over 200,000 ducats when he died, his salary from the Sultan having been supplemented by gifts from European ambassadors (Gürkan, 2015: 114).

Commercial brokers also provided vital linguistic mediation. In Venice, for example, the guild of brokers (known as *sanseri* or *sensali*) admitted only citizens, but many migrants to the city were given special privileges to work as brokers or did so illicitly, including numerous Jews, Greeks, Armenians, and Germans. Individuals like Giulio Torquato, a redeemed slave who had spent twelve years in Constantinople and was granted brokerage rights to work with Ottoman traders, used their experiences of mobility and knowledge of multiple foreign languages to aid their interactions with foreign merchants (Rothman, 2011: 55–6).

The 'new diplomatic history' has highlighted the vital role of mobile figures such as renegades, Jewish merchants, and sailors in mediating informally between different parties and carrying messages across linguistic and cultural barriers (Gürkan, 2015; Van Gelder & Krstić, 2015; cf. also Iordannou, 2019; De Vivo, 2019). As Rizzi writes, 'their experience of mobility, together with their rhetorical claims about their own trustworthiness, made it possible for strangers, slaves, or renegades to be trusted, at least temporarily, for strategic reasons' (2021: 55). As well as being crucial vectors of political and commercial knowledge, diplomats and their secretaries also were key figures in collecting, translating, and transmitting to wider audiences ethnographic and geographical information about distant lands, such as some of the first Spanish texts about the New World (Horodowich, 2018: 33, 83).

A great many Renaissance interpreters and translators were thus semi-professionals or amateurs. Again and again, we can note how their personal experiences of travel or migration were crucial to their work, as in the case of the Huguenot Pierre Coste who produced French translations of works by Locke and Newton while in exile in England (Burke, 2007). Another notable example is the printer John Wolfe who, while he does not appear to have been a translator himself, had spent time working in Florence for local publishers before producing English editions of works by Machiavelli and Aretino, translated by Italian scholars living in London (Massai, 2005). Christian missionaries who spread out across the globe in the Renaissance also were very active linguistic intermediaries, like the many Jesuits who translated Christian (and other) texts into Chinese and other languages (Rubiés, 2017).

Europeans who travelled to different foreign regions also were utterly dependant on local or Indigenous people as linguistic and cultural go-betweens. Among the most famous were women such as the Native American Pocahontas and La Malinche, the enslaved woman who became the interpreter and mistress of the Spanish conquistador Hernán Cortés (Spoturno, 2014; cf. also Metcalf, 2005; Das et al., 2021: 51–6, 148–156). As Greenblatt emphasizes, 'in all [Cortes'] dealings with the peoples of the Yucatán and Mexico [La Malinche] was his principal access to language – at once his tongue and his ears – and hence the key to his hope for survival and success' (1991: 145). Elsewhere, too, the dominance of Europeans was underpinned by the linguistic skills of local people. Even decades after the establishment of their trading post in Macau, for example, most Portuguese merchants remained heavily reliant on their Chinese-born slaves, servants, and wives to operate locally (Gebhardt, 2014).

In Europe, a knowledge of foreign languages could make even the most humble migrant a valuable resource. In Livorno, translating was among the various kinds of informal work that Muslim slaves were allowed to perform during the off-season, when they were not needed as galley rowers. In great trading cities, numerous foreign slaves, such as those from the Black Sea working in Renaissance Venice or the many Black Africans employed in the households of Lisbon, likely provided useful linguistic and cultural guidance to their merchant masters (McKee, 2008; Lowe, 2015). Slaves and servants could also act as interpreters in travelling entourages, while elite travellers might choose to hire local servants to help them learn foreign languages and navigate local customs (Gallagher, 2019; Verhoeven, 2019).

If some low-born linguistic 'go-betweens' achieved high status and renown, their work giving them access to 'mobility, information, and power' (Metcalf, 2005: 3), at the same time navigating between different languages, places, and political regimes put them in a delicate, and vulnerable, position. The very mobility, adaptability, and 'in-betweenness' that gave them valuable skills as intermediaries also made it challenging for them to establish trust and achieve security (Das et al., 2021: 155). At times, linguistic mediators even faced mortal danger when they were made scapegoats for episodes of cross-cultural conflict or misunderstanding (Bonnotte-Hoover, 2021; Rizzi, 2021). For this reason among others, other notable translators and interpreters were more stationary, such as the Indian physicians who were vital in the transmission of botanical and medical knowledge from Asia to Europe in the seventeenth century. In their case, staying in one place made it easier for them to build up networks of relations built on familiarity, rendering them more trusted as intellectual collaborators (Raj, 2016).

3.3 Innkeepers, Lodging-house Keepers, Postmasters

Finally, we can turn to look at some other, more settled figures who – even if many had their own histories of migration or travel – also were able to act as significant linguistic and cultural brokers precisely because they occupied strategic locations that brought them into constant contact with others on the move. Section 1 highlighted the role of spaces of hospitality in enabling, but also helping to control, Renaissance mobility. Here, I examine in more detail how the people who provided this hospitality were able to act as agents of exchange, before briefly touching on the related profession of the postmaster.

As demonstrated by the case of Paolina Briani, hospitality was an area in which women featured prominently. A great many women, including many widows, made their living offering accommodation within their own houses, as well as food and drink, thereby supporting their families or supplementing their income from other work. In Rome in 1517, for example, nearly 90 per cent of lodging houses were run by women (Romani, 1948: 72; see also Canepari, 2014; Bernardi & Pompermaier, 2019). There could be overlap between lodging houses and the sex industry, the writer Pietro Aretino suggesting that taking lodgers was a common career choice for retired courtesans (2005: 108). But many other professions pursued this kind of work on the side. In university towns, male scholars and professors might also engage in the business of renting rooms to foreign students, as did Galileo Galilei himself when he held the chair of mathematics in Padua (Ronchi, 1967: 302). Many migrants, who might have faced difficulties accessing certain professions controlled by local guilds, offered lodging as an occupation. Renting out rooms to compatriots, with whom one might share a language, dialect, or religion, could be an especially attractive option. In this way, migrants capitalized on their experiences of mobility to make a living in a new place (Salzberg, 2019).

Lodging-house keepers, both women and men, provided useful information or services to their guests but might also mediate in more serious personal conflicts and crises. An interesting example of this is the commercial broker

Francesco Litino, who hailed from Greece and let rooms to Ottoman and Greek merchants in his house close to Venice's port area in the second half of the sixteenth century, as well as acting as an unofficial interpreter because of his knowledge of Greek and Slavic as well as Venetian dialects. His house came to the attention of the Venetian Inquisition when a Bosnian servant escaped his patrician employer, converted to Islam, and hid out there, waiting to hop on a boat to Constantinople. Although Litino claimed ignorance of the apostasy, the convert was aided by a Muslim merchant lodger in the house, as well as by Litino's children and his wife Giulia, a migrant from Dalmatia who would continue to manage the lodging house after her husband's death.[26] This and other Inquisition cases, such as the investigation of Paolina Briani, reveal how the sometimes intimate sharing of domestic space in lodging houses, often over longer periods of time than one might spend at an inn, could lead to complex and occasionally fraught encounters between house keepers, tenants, family members, and neighbours. Numerous kinds of exchanges took place as meals were shared, conversations pursued, and books and ideas swapped. At the same time, conflict and misunderstanding were not unusual. When a Muslim Turkish lodger offered some food to Litino's four-year-old daughter, for example, her mother forbade her to eat it; fearing that the unfamiliar dish might contravene fasting restrictions, she gave the morsel to the cat instead. Ultimately, whether they were settled migrants or long-established natives, it is clear that lodging-house keepers acted as vital intersection points within and between larger networks of migrants, travellers, and locals. Negotiating differences of language and custom, they smoothed the passages of mobile people and, in some instances, their gradual integration into new communities.

Many of the same things could be said about innkeepers, who have been described as 'link[ing] the local and the global in early modern society' (Kümin, 2007: 122). Innkeepers walked an especially fine line as intermediaries between their foreign guests and local authorities and customers. Their function as go-betweens was compounded, and indeed often assisted, by the fact that, again, many of them were migrants, such as the numerous German hosts in Siena or the Italians in Avignon (Coulet, 1982). Their foreignness could be an advantage, allowing them to use their knowledge of languages and experience of travel to understand the needs of their customers. At the same time, like other figures discussed already in this section, the innkeepers' position was an ambiguous one, and they too often aroused suspicion or resentment, with Renaissance

---

[26] Archivio di stato, Venice, Sant'uffizio, busta 35, fasc. 12. For more on this case, see Salzberg (2019); Burke (2013); Rothman (2011: chap. 1).

literature including numerous depictions of innkeepers as swindlers and frauds (Tuliani, 1994: 106).

Innkeepers frequently were the first port of call for anyone arriving in a town or village and seeking news, information, or orientation of some kind. A German traveller in Switzerland in 1474, for example, requested help from the innkeeper when he wanted to find his way to meet a local hermit. The host lent him a horse and put him in touch with a priest who, after dinner at the inn, promised to take him to his destination (Kümin & Tlusty, 2011: II, 293). Having viewed the magnificent paintings in Venice's Ducal Palace, a Dutch pilgrim asked his innkeeper about them; the host responded by giving him a printed pamphlet on the historical subject of one of the paintings, which the traveller then translated and transcribed into his diary (Toffolo, 2022). As well as providing information about local sites, innkeepers were essential facilitators of commercial exchanges, and not just for the many merchants and traders who passed through their establishments. We find them acting as witnesses on contracts signed in their premises, exchanging currencies, offering credit in return for pawned goods, or helping to organize onward transport (Kümin, 2007: 96–8). Such transactions often led to conflict and disputes, as in the case of one guest at an inn in sixteenth-century Cologne who ran up such a bill that he had to leave his horses and other belongings as surety and eventually ended up in court with the innkeeper after his possessions were sold (Kümin & Tlusty, 2011: II, 306).

Renaissance innkeepers, moreover, have been described as 'the backbone of policies aiming to control the movements and presence of foreigners in the territory' (Canepari, 2012: 112). They were often required, as discussed in Section 1, to submit daily lists of their arriving and departing guests and were ordered to refuse to accommodate undesirable migrants such as foreign beggars (Coy, 2008; Salzberg, 2018). Innkeepers also were meant to ensure that their establishments did not become havens for seditious talk, immoral behaviour, or the spread of disease. In seventeenth-century Bern, for example, hosts had to swear an oath:

> if they hear, suspect or learn of something in or outside their public houses in words or deeds, which could be detrimental, damaging or disadvantageous to their rulers' standing and reputation (or that of their officials), to notify them … not to consciously accommodate suspicious persons, whores and rogues, particularly not people infected by the French or other serious diseases … not to tolerate (or accommodate) shameless and scandalous things. (Kümin & Tlusty, 2011: III, 8)

Their significant role in ensuring stability and security in their establishments led to the close supervision of innkeepers, often by means of professional corporations which forced them to adhere to numerous regulations (Fanfani, 1936; Romani, 1948: chap. 3). Incorporation encouraged the increasing specialization and professionalization of a trade which previously had often been a sideline or a second or third job alongside other work such as brewing.

While most innkeepers were men (women comprising only 14 per cent of guild members in mid-fourteenth-century Florence, for example), nonetheless there was a good number of women working in inns, including the wives or widows of male publicans (Coulet, 1982: 198; cf. Kümin, 2007: 61–2). Although rarely officially in charge, women played a vital part in the reception and entertainment of guests as well as in the oversight of food and accommodation provision. In the Lyons inn depicted by the humanist Erasmus, for example, 'a woman was always standing by the table to enliven the meal with jokes and pleasantries', the hostess being followed by 'her daughter, a lovely woman with such delightful manners and speech that she could cheer Cato himself' (1997: 370). Unsurprisingly, women working in inns, whether independent landladies, the wives and daughters of innkeepers, or young female servants, also were seen as potential participants in sexual exchange. While travelling through Bavaria on his way to an Imperial Diet in the early sixteenth century, the Florentine ambassador Vettori reported with relish that the hostess of the inn where he stayed had gone to bed with a priest while her husband played games in the lounge. At another Bavarian inn, the servant of a Spanish prelate broke into the room of the innkeeper's granddaughter at night, while elsewhere it was supposedly the host's daughter who snuck into the bed of a guest whom she found appealing (Kümin & Tlusty, 2011: II, 295).

Inns also were crucial hubs in the expanding postal network in this period, with some innkeepers doubling as postmasters. However, the postmaster too would emerge as an increasingly defined professional figure in the Renaissance, overseeing the rapid relay between mounted messengers as well as the renting of horses to travellers for their onward journeys (Midura, 2020). A critical stage in the development of this network took place from the 1490s, when Holy Roman Emperor Maximilian I gave the Taxis (Tassi) family from the Bergamo region in northern Italy the task of managing the new imperial postal service that ran regularly between Innsbruck and Brussels, linking these key nodes in the Habsburg domain. Members of the Taxis family gained wealth and even noble titles from their roles as postmaster general of various branches of the Imperial post over the next two centuries. Meanwhile, the more organized post continued to run alongside other, older courier services such as those operated by monasteries or universities or within merchant networks. Venice's own courier system naturally also extended eastwards, towards Dalmatia (by boat) and Constantinople (overland), while Seville was the only European port licensed to carry mail to the Indies (Dursteler, 2009; Behringer, 2003; Schobesberger et al., 2016). The evolution of these postal systems in the fifteenth and sixteenth centuries has been described as an unheralded revolution which radically changed the transmission of news, paved the way for the full emergence of a public sphere, altered the conduct of business, and facilitated a burgeoning culture of correspondence. The speed and frequency of cross-border intellectual and artistic exchanges that characterized the 'Renaissance of Letters' was underwritten by this infrastructure (Findlen & Sutherland, 2019). The provision of regular transport services from post stations made mobility around the continent easier and faster while, at the same time, enabling European authorities a greater level of surveillance over the movement of both people and information, as suggested by an early postal map of France by the royal cartographer under Louis XIII (Figure 12).

Alongside the management of the material infrastructure of transport and hospitality, we also see postmasters directing more ephemeral flows of information. 'The nodal points of the postal system automatically became places where news was received and sent on', as individual postmasters subscribed to printed and manuscript newsletters and played a role in diffusing them

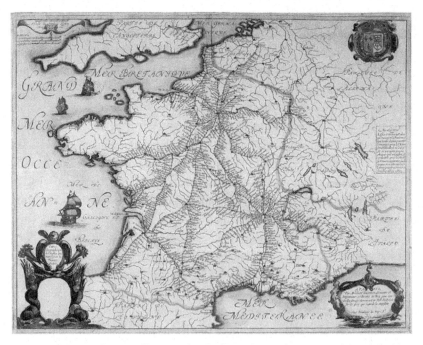

Figure 12 Postal map of France by the French royal cartographer Nicholas Sanson, showing the dense network of postal roads and stations, 1632. By permission of the Bibliothèque nationale de France.

(Schobesberger et al., 2016: 29–30). As mentioned in Section 2, Ottavio Codogno, the Milanese deputy postmaster general in the early seventeenth century, was the author of one of the most important printed postal itineraries. But he also allegedly used his position to gather intelligence for the Spanish governor of Milan, by intercepting the letters carried by Venetian couriers. It is also noteworthy that Codogno, who was of humble birth and possibly a migrant from the Spanish Netherlands, worked closely with Lucina Cattanea Tassis, who took over the role of postmistress of Milan in 1599 after the death of her husband. Far from holding the office in name only, Tassis actively oversaw a network of around fifteen couriers and twenty subordinate postmasters across Northern Italy. And she was not the only woman to do so: another widow from the same family, Lucia Ropele Taxis Bordogna, was the postmistress at Trento in the mid-seventeenth century, commissioning a portrait of herself depicted sorting the mail destined for various destinations across Europe, despite the fact that she was reputed to be illiterate (Midura, 2020: chap. 4).

Returning to where we began at the start of this section, however, with more itinerant professions, it is also important to remember the vital work of couriers in disseminating letters, goods, and news (sometimes unofficially, because of indiscretions or the robbery of their mailbags) as they moved around the postal network (Midura, 2019). Couriers and other messengers had to be mobility experts to cope with the dangers of the road, from ambushes to bad weather to plague, and often travelled in groups for security. As well as being highly mobile by necessity, they too might have longer histories of migration, such as the migrants from the Brembana valley near Bergamo who monopolized the Venetian company of couriers (*Mariegola*, 2001), providing yet another example of how different types of mobility intersected and reinforced each other in this period.

Whether operating professionally or informally, all kinds of ordinary migrants and travellers acted as critical transmitters of information and ideas in the Renaissance and as intermediaries in a great range of productive exchanges. Other highly mobile groups might easily be mentioned in this regard, from medical charlatans (Gentilcore, 2006) to galley convicts (Reeves, 2021), soldiers (Martinez, 2016) to seamen (Carey, 2019). Many mobile people can seem marginal and insignificant if we only study them from a static perspective, where they constantly slip from our view. But if we can find ways to follow their paths, many reveal themselves to have been critical agents of exchange, without whom Renaissance culture would not have spread nor developed in the same way. Drawing on their experiences of travel, their familiarity with multiple languages and dialects, and their flexibility in adopting different roles and positions, figures such as the ones examined in this section were instrumental to the cross-cultural encounters that gave this period so much of its creative energy – not to mention, in some cases, literally putting their bodies on the line to transmit commodities or messages.

At the same time, we have seen how people with a history of mobility and/or a liminal position as mediators between cultures and languages frequently encountered hostility and suspicion both from local authorities and from settled communities – and how they might have a hard time establishing reputation and trust. This could be because they threatened to take work from locals or to become a burden on community resources, but it could also be owing to the widespread anxiety that people who came from elsewhere, or who moved constantly, might carry along with them dangerous things, from deadly pathogens to heretical ideas. As well as curiosity, benevolence, and the quest for profit, exchanges in this period were fundamentally shaped by fear, resentment, and prejudice. And yet, it is important to remember in turn that these same attitudes towards those from other places also spurred even more people into motion over long distances: setting armies on the march, or contributing to the eradication, expulsion, or enslavement of groups of 'others'. In other words, it was precisely the more intolerant, violent aspects of the period which led to sometimes unexpected and unintended episodes of cross-cultural encounter and exchange, and these various strands cannot be easily disentangled.

Conclusion

> *When I return I will amaze the whole gang, and I hope that at that time a large crowd will come up to greet me, with the sound of tambourines, bells, and pipes, crying 'Long live our great and excellent Doctor, who will be the pride of our valley. This is the very Zanni, who by studying for days, months, and years, has made the Bergamask valley famous.' (Dui bellissimi sonetti, 1580)*

With these words, the popular performance character Zanni, put forward at the beginning of this Element as an exemplary Renaissance migrant, fantasized about his return to his rural home after a time spent working in the great metropolis of Venice. In a second pamphlet from the same period, another Zanni-type character lived up to the reputation of the *bergamaschi* as constant travellers in search of a better life, while also showing off his ignorance of geography; he recounted his voyage to Calicut via the Casentino valley in Tuscany, to Spain and then Padua, and to the region around Verona where the legendary Christian king Prester John supposedly lived (*Un viazo*, ca. 1550). The joke of popular works like these was precisely that such characters were *not* turned into sophisticates by their extensive travels or their time in the city, despite their illusions to be so. Their rough rural accents, unworldliness, and bad attempts at speaking Italian or Latin were meant to make very plain that they remained uneducated hicks, a fact that travel and urban experience could not change (Salzberg, 2017).

We can compare this with another perspective from the same time and the same region. In his 1564 compendium *Concerning the Mirror of Universal Knowledge* (*Dello specchio di scientia universale . . .*), the Bolognese physician and charlatan Leonardo Fioravanti described his own travels across Italy as well as around the Mediterranean to Croatia, Spain, and North Africa:

> I went seeking truth in many parts of the world, and I learned this truth
> from different sorts of people and from the animals and the plants of
> the earth . . . so as not to walk blindly as many do for not having walked
> about the world and witnessed the great diversity of things of nature, as
> I have seen in the great amount of time that I went traveling about the
> earth, sailing through the sea, and experiencing maritime and land wars . . .
> *(quoted in Biow, 2015: 123)*[27]

In other words, Fioravanti argued that it was precisely his highly itinerant past that gave him greater authority than a sedentary scholar who absorbed knowledge only from books, vindicating the power of mobility to generate knowledge and new perspectives.

Such works remind us of some of the tension and ambivalence surrounding mobility in this period, of which I have given numerous other examples. Migration and travel did not automatically lead to the development of a cosmopolitan outlook or increased tolerance of difference, neither on the part of people on the move nor of the communities that hosted them, whether for a brief stay or a long one (cf. Jacob, 2006). Nor were all the exchanges that mobility engendered harmonious, creative, or beneficial to both parties. Rather they reflected the inequalities inherent to European Renaissance society, and many played out in instances of discrimination, violence, theft, and exploitation. As we have seen, the growing number and variety of people on the roads also fuelled intolerance, suspicion, increased controls on movement, and attempts to distinguish welcome from unwelcome arrivals. These reactions had a marked impact on the experiences of migrants and travellers, especially on the poor and members of ethnic or religious minorities. As Europe became progressively more connected over the course of the period, it was at the same time ever more riven by divisions. War, religious schism, and disease (especially plague) also enforced moments of rupture and temporary stasis, breaks in

---

[27] On the fascinating figure of Fioravanti, who also faced continuous criticism and attacks, see also Camporesi (1997).

the system and damage to fundamental infrastructures, as various kinds of mobility were halted or impeded, at least for a time.

This interplay between mobility and immobility, and the constant tension between the risks, costs, and benefits of allowing people to move over space, should be recognized as a central dynamic of Renaissance culture. Drawing out this dynamic casts new light on the well-known aspects and characters of the period while also revealing its more obscure corners. As well as being simply a necessity for many people who needed to find work or escape danger, the accelerating movement of people fundamentally shaped the culture of the time, whether by helping to spread and standardize ideas and practices or by producing new, hybrid mixtures that often amounted to more than the sum of their parts. Mobility has long been recognized as an essential aspect of the careers of many leading Renaissance figures, from Erasmus to Michelangelo. At the same time, the experiences of such exceptional individuals need to be viewed in the context of the period's broader panorama of movement and of the practices and infrastructures that shaped it.

In particular, this Element has emphasized the need to consider the practical, spatial, and material aspects of moving in this period. Future research might consider more how face-to-face interactions between people on the move and local communities were shaped by the contours of spaces like inns, lodging houses, coaches, and ships, as well as courts, guild halls, town squares, and marketplaces. It might examine further the infrastructure of communication (facilities for sending letters, receiving news, conveying gifts or goods) to get to grips with how exchanges of knowledge and information took place. And it might reflect more on what kinds of material and immaterial things actually were exchanged as people moved: money, merchandise, letters, books, artworks, antiquities, food, and diseases, but also words, languages, ideas, customs, skills, news, hospitality, kindness, and hostility. These approaches can help us discern the effects of mobility both on mobile people and on the societies that they passed through or settled in; to see what facilitated, or impeded, different kinds of cultural exchange and how, in practice, migrants and travellers helped to create and to transmit Renaissance culture.

Bibliography

Archival Sources

Archivio di Stato, Florence
  Arte dei medici e speziali
Archivio di Stato, Venice
  Giustizia Nuova
  Sant'Uffizio

Printed Primary Sources

Aretino, Pietro. (2005). *Aretino's Dialogues*, trans. Raymond Rosenthal. University of Toronto Press.

Boccaccio, Giovanni. (2012). *Decameron*, ed. Romualdo Marrone & Franco Cardini. Rome: Newton Compton.

Bottani, Tarcisio, and Wanda Taufer, eds. (2001). *Mariegola. Della Compagnia dei corrieri. Della Serenissima signoria*. Bergamo: Corponove.

Camporesi, Piero, ed. (2007). *Il libro dei vagabondi. Lo* Speculum Cerretanorum *di Teseo Pini,* Il Vagabondo *di Rafaele Frianoro e altri testi di 'furfanteria'* . Milan: Garzanti; first published 1973.

Cellini, Benvenuto. (1995). *The Life of Benvenuto Cellini*, trans. John Addington Symons. London: Phaidon Press; first published 1951.

Disgrazie del Zane, narrate in un sonetto di diciasete linguazi, come giungendo ad una hostaria certi banditi il volsero amazar. No bibliographic information. Biblioteca Universitaria Alessandrina, Rome, Misc. XIII.a.57.13.

Dui bellissimi sonetti in lingua bergamascha . . . Venice: Al Segno della Regina, 1580. In *La Commedia dell'Arte*, ed. Pandolfi, 1: 198–204.

Erasmus, Desiderius. (1997). 'Diversoria', 369–80. In his *Colloquies*, trans. and annotated Craig R. Thompson, *Collected Works of Erasmus*, vol. 40. University of Toronto Press.

Fabri, Felix. (1896). *Felix Fabri (circa 1480–1483 A.D.)*, trans. Aubrey Stewart, vol. I, part 1. The Library of the Palestine Pilgrims' Text Society. London Committee of the Palestine Exploration Fund.

Fontana, Bartolomeo. (1995). *Itinerari. Edizione critica di Robert C. Melzi, con uno studio su 'Due viaggiatori veneziani attraverso l'Europa del Cinquecento'*. Geneva: Slatkine.

Lotto, Lorenzo. (2017). *Lorenzo Lotto. Il libro di spese diverse*, ed. Francesco De Carolis. Edizioni Università di Trieste.

Montaigne, Michel de. (2003). 'Travel Journal', 1049–1270. In his *The Complete Works*, trans. Donald M. Frame. New York: Everyman's Library.

Moryson, Fynes. (1617). *An Itinerary Containing his Ten Yeeres Travell* ... 2 vols. London: John Beale.

Pandolfi, Vito, ed. (1957). *La Commedia dell'Arte. Storia e testo*, 6 vols. Florence: Sansoni Antiquariato.

Sanudo, Marin. (1879–1903). *I diarii di Marino Sanuto*, ed. Rinaldo Fulin, Federico Stefani, Nicolò Barozzi, et al., 58 vols. Venice: R. Deputazione Veneta di Storia Patria.

Simonsfeld, Henry, ed. (1903). 'Itinerario de Germania delli magnifici ambasciatori veneti, M. Giorgio Contarini, conte del Zaffo, et M. Polo Pisani ... dell'anno 1492', 275–345. In *Miscellanea di storia veneta*, ed. Henry Simonsfeld. Venice: Deputazione Veneta di Storia Patria.

Un viazo che ha fatto misser Pedrol bergamasco qual narra li paesi che lha visto ... [Venice, ca. 1550]. British Library, 1071.c.65(3).

Vasari, Giorgio. (1912–15). *Lives of the Most Eminent Painters Sculptors and Architects*, trans. Gaston du C. De Vere, 10 vols. London: Philip Lee Warner.

Vesalius, Andreas. (1950). *The Illustrations from the Works of Andreas Vesalius of Brussels*, trans. and annotated J. B. de C. M. Saunders and Charles D. O'Malley. Mineola, NY: Dover Publishing.

Viaggio de Zan Padella, cosa ridiculosa e bela, dond es descrif tug le cose ches vende sul punt de Rialt in Venesia. Modena [ca. 1580]. British Library, 1071.c.63(20).

Printed Secondary Sources

Adey, Peter et al., eds. (2014). *The Routledge Handbook of Mobilities*. New York: Routledge.

Akhimie, Patricia, and Bernadette Andrea, eds. (2019). *Travel and Travail: Early Modern Women, English Drama, and the Wider World*. Lincoln: University of Nebraska Press.

Arbel, Benjamin. (2017). 'Daily Life on Board Venetian Ships: The Evidence of Renaissance Travelogues and Diaries'. In Gherardo Ortalli and Alessio Sopracasa, eds., *Rapporti mediterranei, pratiche documentarie, presenze veneziane: Le reti economiche e culturali (xiv–xvi secolo)*. Venice: Istituto Veneto di Scienze, Lettere ed Arti, 183–220.

Aslanian, Sebouh D. (2020). 'The "Quintessential Locus of Brokerage": Letters of Recommendation, Networks, and Mobility in the Life of Thomas Vanandets'i, an Armenian Printer in Amsterdam, 1677–1707'. *Journal of World History*, 31, 4: 655–92.

Aslanian, Sebouh D. (2019). '"Many Have Come Here and Have Deceived Us": Some Notes on Asateur Vardapet (1644–1728), an Itinerant Armenian Monk in Europe'. *Zeitschrift für Armenische Philologie*, 132: 133–94.

Aslanian, Sebouh D. (2014). 'Port Cities and Printers: Reflections on Early Modern Global Armenian Print Culture'. *Book History*, 17: 51–93.

Bale, Anthony, and Kathryne Beebe. (2021). 'Pilgrimage and Textual Culture'. *Journal of Medieval and Early Modern Studies*, 51, 1: 1–8.

Bamji, Alex. (2019). 'Health Passes, Print and Public Health in Early Modern Europe'. *Social History of Medicine*, 32, 3: 441–64.

Barker, Hannah. (2019). *That Most Precious Merchandise: The Mediterranean Trade in Black Sea Slaves, 1260–1500*. Philadelphia: University of Pennsylvania Press.

Behringer, Wolfgang. (2006). 'Communications Revolutions: A Historiographical Concept'. *German History*, 24, 3: 333–74.

Behringer, Wolfgang. (2003). *Im Zeichen des Merkur: Reichspost und Kommunikationsrevolution in der frühen Neuzeit*. Göttingen: Vandenhoeck & Ruprecht.

Bellavitis, Anna. (2006). 'Apprentissages masculins, apprentissages féminins à Venise au xvie siècle'. *Histoire urbaine*, 1, 15: 49–73.

Benner, Erica. (2017). *Be Like the Fox: Machiavelli's Lifelong Quest for Freedom*. New York: W. W. Norton.

Bernardi, Teresa, and Matteo Pompermaier. (2019). 'Hospitality and Registration of Foreigners in Early Modern Venice: The Role of Women within Inns and Lodging Houses'. *Gender & History*, 31, 3: 624–45.

Betteridge, Thomas, ed. (2007). *Borders and Travellers in Early Modern Europe*. Aldershot: Ashgate.

Bianchi, Francesco, and Deborah Howard. (2003). 'Life and Death in Damascus: The Material Culture of Venetians in the Syrian Capital in the Mid-Fifteenth Century'. *Studi veneziani*, 16: 233–301.

Bilic, Darka. (2023). '"Even if the Sultan of Turkey Came They Would Have to Put Him in Quarantine": Commercial Lazarettos in the Adriatic in the Sixteenth Century'. In Nelles and Salzberg, *Connected Mobilities*, 157–82.

Biow, Douglas. (2015). *On the Importance of Being an Individual in Renaissance Italy: Men, Their Professions, and Their Beards*. Philadelphia: University of Pennsylvania Press, 117–151. https://doi.org/10.9783/9780812290509

Blazina Tomic, Zlata, and Vesna Blazina. (2015). *Expelling the Plague: The Health Office and the Implementation of Quarantine in Dubrovnik, 1377–1533*. Montreal: McGill–Queen's University Press.

Boccagni, Paolo, and Loretta Baldassar. (2015). 'Emotions on the Move: Mapping the Emergent Field of Emotion and Migration'. *Emotion, Space and Society*, 16: 73–80. https://doi.org/10.1016/j.emospa.2015.06.009

Boes, Maria R. (2007). 'Unwanted Travellers: The Tightening of City Borders in Early Modern Germany'. In Betteridge, *Borders and Travellers*, 87–112.

Bonnotte-Hoover, Céline. (2021). 'Language, Mediation, Conflict and Power in Early Modern China: The Roles of the Interpreter in Matteo Ricci's Journals'. In Gelléri and Willie, *Travel and Conflict*, 39–51.

Braunstein, Philippe. (2016). *Les allemands à Venise (1380–1520)*. Rome: École Française de Rome.

Brayshay, Mark. (2005). 'Waits, Musicians, Bearwards and Players: The Inter-urban Road Travel and Performances of Itinerant Entertainers in Sixteenth and Seventeenth Century England'. *Journal of Historical Geography*, 31, 3: 430–58.

Brizio, Elena. (2021). '"Ben venga Carlo imperadore!": Welcoming the Enemy to Siena in 1536'. In Goldstein and Piana, *Early Modern Hospitality*, 41–61.

Broomhall, Susan. (2019). 'Cross-Channel Affections: Pressure and Persuasion in Letters to Calvinist Refugees in England, 1569–1570'. In Giovanni Tarantino and Charles Zika, eds. *Religious Conflict, Exile and Emotions in Early Modern Europe*. London: Routledge, 27–43.

Brotton, Jerry. (2002). *The Renaissance Bazaar: From the Silk Road to Michelangelo*. Oxford: Oxford University Press.

Buono, Alessandro. (2015). 'La manutenzione dell'identità. Il riconoscimento degli eredi legittimi nello stato di Milano e nella repubblica di Venezia (secoli XVII e XVIII)'. *Quaderni Storici*, 50, 148: 231–65.

Burke, Ersie. (2013). 'Francesco di Demetri Litino, the Inquisition and the Fondaco Dei Turchi'. *Thesaurismata*, 36: 79–96.

Burke, Peter. (2017). *Exiles and Expatriates in the History of Knowledge, 1500–2000. The Menahem Stern Jerusalem Lectures*. Waltham, MA: Brandeis University Press.

Burke, Peter. (2007). 'Cultures of Translation in Early Modern Europe'. In Burke and Hsia, *Cultural Translation*, 7–38. http://doi:10.1017/CBO9780511497193.002

Burke, Peter, and Ronnie P. Hsia, eds. (2007). *Cultural Translation in Early Modern Europe*. Cambridge: Cambridge University Press. http://doi:10.1017/CBO9780511497193

Calabi, Donatella, and Stephen Turk Christensen, eds. (2007). *Cities and Cultural Exchange in Europe, 1400–1700*. Vol. 2 of *Cultural Exchange in Early Modern Europe*. Cambridge: Cambridge University Press/European Science Foundation.

Calaresu, Melissa. (2020). 'Street "Luxuries" in Early Modern Rome'. In Sarah Carter and Ivan Gaskell, eds., *The Oxford Handbook of History and Material Culture*. Oxford: Oxford University Press, 1–27.

Calis, Richard. (2019). 'Reconstructing the Ottoman Greek World: Early Modern Ethnography in the Household of Martin Crusius'. *Renaissance Quarterly*, 72, 1: 148–93. http://doi:10.1017/rqx.2018.4

Calvi, Giulia. (2022). *The World in Dress: Costume Books across Italy, Europe, and the East*. Cambridge Elements in the Renaissance. Cambridge: Cambridge University Press. https://doi.org/10.1017/9781108913829

Camporesi, Pietro. (1997). *Camminare il mondo: vita e avventure di Leonardo Fioravanti, medico del Cinquecento*. Milan: Garzanti.

Canepari, Eleanora. (2014). 'Cohabitations, Household Structures and Gender Identities in Seventeenth-Century Rome'. *Villa I Tatti Studies*, 17: 131–54. https://doi.org/10.1086/675766

Canepari, Eleanora. (2013). 'Women on Their Way: Employment Opportunities in Cosmopolitan Rome'. In Anne Montenach and Deborah Simonton, eds., *Female Agency in the Eighteenth-Century Economy, Gender in Towns, 1640–1830*. London: Routledge, 206–23.

Canepari, Eleanora. (2012). 'Who is Not Welcome? Reception and Rejection of Migrants in Early Modern Italian Cities'. In De Munck and Winter, *Gated Communities*, 105–15.

Canny, Nicholas, ed. (1994). *Europeans on the Move: Studies on European Migration, 1500–1800*. Oxford: Oxford University Press.

Capp, Bernard. (1994). *The World of John Taylor the Water-Poet*. Oxford: Clarendon Press.

Cappa, Desirée. (2022). 'Pierfrancesco Riccio: The Rise of a Bureaucrat in the Service of the Medici Family (1525–44)'. PhD thesis, Warburg Institute, University of London.

Caramel, Niccolò. (2019). 'Rapporti commerciali, organizzazione dei viaggi, ripercussioni locali: nuove prospettive sull'ambulantato tesino (1685–1797).' *Studi trentini*, 98, 1: 155–84.

Carey, Daniel. (2019). 'The Problem of Credibility in Early Modern Travel'. In Holmberg, *Renaissance and Early Modern Travel*, 524–47. https://doi.org/10.1111/rest.12567

Carnevali, Rebecca. (2020). 'Cheap, Everyday Print: Jobbing Printing and its Users in Post-Tridentine Bologna'. PhD thesis, University of Warwick.

Cassen, Flora. (2019). 'Jewish Travelers in Early Modern Italy: Visible and Invisible Resistance to the Jewish Badge'. In Denise Klein and Thomas Weller, eds., *Dress and Cultural Difference in Early Modern Europe*. Berlin: De Gruyter Oldenbourg, 73–89.

Ceriotti, Luca, and Federica Dallasta. (2009). 'Lutero sulle spalle. Colportage e diffusione dell'iconografia protestante in un processo del 1558'. *Aurea Parma*, 93: 405–22.

Chojnacka, Monica. (2001). *Working Women of Early Modern Venice*. Baltimore, MD: Johns Hopkins University Press.

Cipolla, Carlo M. (1972). 'The Diffusion of Innovations in Early Modern Europe'. *Comparative Studies in Society and History*, 14, 1: 46–52.

Ciriacono, Salvatore. (2005). 'Migration, Minorities, and Technology Transfer in Early Modern Europe'. *Journal of European Economic History*, 34: 43–64.

Cohen, Thomas V. (2021). 'Hospitality Between the Sheets'. In Goldstein and Piana, *Early Modern Hospitality*, 299–319.

Constable, Olivia. (2006). *Housing the Stranger in the Mediterranean World: Lodging, Trade, and Travel in Late Antiquity and the Middle Ages*. Cambridge: Cambridge University Press; first published 2003.

Costantini, Massimo. (1996). 'Le strutture dell'ospitalità'. In Alberto Tenenti and Ugo Tucci, eds., *Storia di Venezia, V. Il Rinascimento: Società ed economica*. Rome: Istituto della Enciclopedia Italiana, 881–911.

Cowan, Alexander F. (2000). 'Foreigners and the City. The Case of the Immigrant Merchant'. In Alexander F. Cowan, ed., *Mediterranean Urban Culture, 1400–1700*. Exeter: University of Exeter Press, 45–55.

Coulet, Noël. (1982). 'Les hotelleries en France et en Italie au bas moyen age'. In Charles Higounet, ed., *L'homme et la route en Europe occidentale au Moyen Âge*. Toulouse: Presses universitaires du Midi, 181–205.

Cox, Virginia. (2016). *A Short History of the Italian Renaissance*. London: I.B. Tauris.

Coy, Jason. (2008). *Strangers and Misfits: Banishment, Social Control, and Authority in Early Modern Germany*. Leiden: Brill.

Craig, Leigh Ann. (2009). *Wandering Women and Holy Matrons: Women as Pilgrims in the Later Middle Ages*. Leiden: Brill.

Dalton, Heather, ed. (2020). *Keeping Family in an Age of Long Distance Trade, Imperial Expansion, and Exile, 1550–1850*. Amsterdam: Amsterdam University Press.

Das, Nandini, ed. (2022). *Lives in Transit in Early Modern England*. Amsterdam: Amsterdam University Press. https://doi.org/10.5117/9789463725989

Das, Nandini, João Vicente Melo, Haig Smith & Lauren Working, eds. (2021). *Keywords of Identity, Race, and Human Mobility in Early Modern England*. Amsterdam: Amsterdam University Press. https://doi .org/10.5117/9789463720748

Davis, Robert C., and Gary R. Marvin. (2004). *Venice, the Tourist Maze: A Cultural Critique of the World's Most Touristed City.* Berkeley: University of California Press.

Degl'Innocenti, Luca, and Massimo Rospocher, eds. (2019a). *Street Singers in Renaissance Europe.* Special Issue of *Renaissance Studies*, 33, 1.

Degl'Innocenti, Luca, and Massimo Rospocher. (2019b). 'Urban Voices: The Hybrid Figure of the Street Singer in Renaissance Italy'. In Degl'Innocenti and Rospocher, *Street Singers*, 17–41.

De Munck, Bert, and Anne Winter, eds. (2012). *Gated Communities: Regulating Migration in Early Modern Cities.* London: Routledge.

De Vivo, Filippo. (2019). 'Microhistories of Long-Distance Information: Space, Movement and Agency in the Early Modern News', *Past & Present*, 242, Issue Supplement 14: 179–214. https://doi.org/10.1093/pastj/gtz042

De Vivo, Filippo. (2016). 'Walking in Sixteenth-Century Venice: Mobilizing the Early Modern City'. *I Tatti Studies in the Italian Renaissance*, 19, 1: 115–41.

Di Lenardo, Isabella. (2018). 'Dürer tra Norimberga e Venezia, 1506–1507'. In Bernard Aikema and Andrew Martin, eds., *Dürer e il rinascimento tra Germania e Italia.* Milan: 24 Ore Cultura, 101–5.

Dursteler, Eric R. (2012). 'Speaking in Tongues: Language and Communication in the Early Modern Mediterranean'. *Past & Present*, 217, 1: 47–77. https://doi.org/10.1093/pastj/gts023

Dursteler, Eric R. (2011). *Renegade Women: Gender, Identity, and Boundaries in the Early Modern Mediterranean.* Baltimore, MD: Johns Hopkins University Press.

Dursteler, Eric R. (2009). 'Power and Information: The Venetian Postal System in the Mediterranean, 1573–1645'. In Diogo Curto et al., eds., *From Florence to the Mediterranean: Studies in Honor of Anthony Molho.* Florence: Olschki, 601–23.

Earle, Rebecca. (2017). 'Climate, Travel and Colonialism in the Early Modern World'. In Sara Miglietti and John Morgan, eds., *Governing the Environment in the Early Modern World: Theory and Practice.* London: Routledge, 22–37.

Ebrahim, Fatima. (2021). 'The Vulnerability of Anglo-Islamic Hospitality in the Early Modern Period'. In Goldstein and Piana, *Early Modern Hospitality*, 357–80.

Eliav-Feldon, Miriam. (2012). *Renaissance Impostors and Proofs of Identity.* New York: Palgrave Macmillan.

Fanfani, Amintore. (1936). 'Note sull'industria alberghiera italiana nel medio evo'. In Amintore Fanfani, *Saggi di storia economica italiana.* Milano: Vita e Pensiero, 111–21.

Faroqhi, Suraiya. (2014). *Travel and Artisans in the Ottoman Empire: Employment and Mobility in the Early Modern Era*. London: I.B. Tauris.

Federici, Federico, and Dario Tessicini, eds. (2014). *Translators, Interpreters, and Cultural Negotiators: Mediating and Communicating Power from the Middle Ages to the Modern Era*. London: Palgrave Macmillan.

Ferraro, Joanne M. (2016). 'Youth in Peril in Early Modern Venice'. *Journal of Social History*, 49, 4: 761–83. https://doi.org/10.1093/jsh/shv075

Ferrone, Siro. (1993). *Attori, mercanti, corsari: La commedia dell'arte in Europa tra Cinque e Seicento*. Turin: Einaudi.

Fietta Ielen, Elda. (1985). *Con la cassela in spalla: gli ambulanti di Tesino*. Ivrea (Turin): Priuli & Verlucca.

Findlen, Paula, and Suzanne Sutherland, eds. (2019). *The Renaissance of Letters: Knowledge and Community in Italy, 1300–1650*. London: Routledge. https://doi.org/10.4324/9780429429774

Fontaine, Laurence. (1996). *History of Pedlars in Europe*, trans. by Vicki Whittaker. Cambridge: Polity.

Fraser, Elisabeth A., ed. (2020). *The Mobility of People and Things in the Early Modern Mediterranean: The Art of Travel*. London: Routledge.

Fumerton, Patricia. (2006). *Unsettled: The Culture of Mobility and the Working Poor in Early Modern England*. Chicago, IL: University of Chicago Press.

Gallagher, John. (2023). 'Linguistic Encounter: Fynes Moryson and the Uses of Language'. In Nelles and Salzberg, *Connected Mobilities*, 41–61.

Gallagher, John. (2019). *Learning Languages in Early Modern England*. Oxford: Oxford University Press.

Gallagher, John. (2017). 'The Italian London of John North: Cultural Contact and Linguistic Encounter in Early Modern England'. *Renaissance Quarterly*, 70: 88–131.

Gebhardt, Jonathan. (2014). 'Negotiating Barriers: Cross-Cultural Communication and the Portuguese Mercantile Community in Macau, 1550–1640'. *Itinerario*, 38, 2: 27–50. http://doi:10.1017/S0165115314000345

Gelléri, Gabor, and Rachel Willie, eds. (2021). *Travel and Conflict in the Early Modern World*. Abingdon: Routledge.

Geltner, Guy. (2019). *Roads to Health: Infrastructure and Urban Wellbeing in Later Medieval Italy*. Philadelphia: University of Pennsylvania Press.

Gentilcore, David. (2006). *Medical Charlatanism in Early Modern Italy*. Oxford: Oxford University Press.

Ghobrial, John-Paul. (2019). 'Moving Stories and What They Tell Us: Early Modern Mobility Between Microhistory and Global History'. *Past & Present*, Supplement 14: 243–80.

Gobel, David. (2018). 'The Inn Outside the City Gate in Early Modern Spain'. Paper delivered at the European Association of Urban History conference, Rome.

Goldstein, David B., and Marco Piana, eds. (2021). *Early Modern Hospitality.* Toronto: Center for Renaissance and Reformation Studies.

Gomis, Juan. (2019). 'Pious Voices: Blind Spanish Prayer Singers'. In Degl'Innocenti and Rospocher, *Street Singers*, 42–63. https://doi.org/10.1111/rest.12533

Gonzalez Martin, Pablo, Rosa Salzberg, and Luca Zenobi, eds. (2021). *Cities in Motion: Mobility and Urban Space in Early Modern Europe.* Special Issue of *Journal of Early Modern History*, 25, 1–2.

Greefs, Hilde, and Anne Winter, eds. (2018). *Migration Policies and Materialities of Identification in European Cities: Papers and Gates, 1500–1930s.* New York: Routledge.

Greenblatt, Stephen. (2010). 'A Mobility Studies Manifesto'. In Stephen Greenblatt, ed. *Cultural Mobility: A Manifesto.* Cambridge: Cambridge University Press, 250–3.

Greenblatt, Stephen. (1991). *Marvellous Possessions: The Wonder of the New World.* Oxford: Clarendon Press.

Griffin, Clive. (2007). 'Itinerant Booksellers, Printers, and Pedlars in Sixteenth-Century Spain and Portugal'. In Robin Myers, Michael Harris, and Giles Mandelbrote, eds., *Fairs, Markets and the Itinerant Book Trade.* London: British Library, 43–59.

Groebner, Valentin. (2007). *Who Are You? Identification, Deception, and Surveillance in Early Modern Europe.* New York: Zone Books.

Gschwend, Annemarie Jordan, and K. J. P. Lowe, eds. (2015). *The Global City: On the Streets of Renaissance Lisbon.* London: Paul Holberton Publishing.

Guerzoni, Guido. (2010). 'Strangers at Home. The Courts of Este Princesses between XVth and XVIIth Centuries'. In Giulia Calvi and Isabella Chabot, eds. *Moving Elites: Women and Cultural Transfers in the European Court System.* Florence: EUI, 141–56.

Guldi, Jo. (2012). *Roads to Power: Britain Invents the Infrastructure State.* Cambridge, MA: Harvard University Press.

Gürkan, Emrah Safa. (2015). 'Mediating Boundaries: Mediterranean Go-Betweens and Cross-Confessional Diplomacy in Constantinople, 1560–1600'. *Journal of Early Modern History*, 19, 2–3: 107–28. https://doi.org/10.1163/15700658-12342453

Hamadeh, Shirine. (2017). 'Invisible City: Istanbul's Migrants and the Politics of Space'. *Eighteenth-Century Studies*, 50, 2: 173–93. http://doi:10.1353/ecs.2017.0002

Harreld, Donald J. (2003). 'Trading Places: The Public and Private Spaces of Merchants in Sixteenth-Century Antwerp'. *Journal of Urban History*, 29, 6: 657–69. https://doi.org/10.1177/0096144203253468

Harms, Roeland, Joad Raymond, and Jeroen Salman, eds. (2013). *Not Dead Things: The Dissemination of Popular Print in England and Wales, Italy, and the Low Countries, 1500–1820*. Leiden: Brill.

Heal, Felicity. (1990). *Hospitality in Early Modern England*. Oxford: Clarendon Press.

Healy, Margaret. (2007). 'Highways, Hospitals and Boundary Hazards'. In Betteridge, *Borders and Travellers*, 18–33.

Heiss, Hans. (2002). 'The Pre-modern Hospitality Trade in the Central Alpine Region: The Example of Tyrol'. In Kümin and Tlusty, *World of the Tavern*, 159–75.

Hell, Maarten. (2014). 'Trade, Transport, and Storage in Amsterdam Inns (1450–1800)'. *Journal of Urban History*, 40, 4: 742–61.

Helmstutler Di Dio, Kelley. (2015). *Making and Moving Sculpture in Early Modern Italy*. London: Taylor & Francis.

Henderson, John. (2019). *Florence Under Siege: Surviving Plague in an Early Modern City*. New Haven, CT: Yale University Press.

Henderson, John. (2006). *The Renaissance Hospital: Healing the Body and Healing the Soul*. New Haven, CT: Yale University Press.

Henke, Robert. (2015). *Poverty and Charity in Early Modern Theatre and Performance*. Iowa City: University of Iowa Press.

Henke, Robert. (1991). 'Border-Crossing in the Commedia dell'arte'. In Eric Nicholson and Robert Henke, eds., *Transnational Exchange in Early Modern Theater*. London: Routledge, 19–34.

Herzig, Tamar. (2019). *A Convert's Tale: Art, Crime, and Jewish Apostasy in Renaissance Italy*. Cambridge, MA: Harvard University Press.

Hewlett, Cecilia. (2016). 'Locating *contadini* in the Renaissance City: Food Circulation and Mobility in the Marketplace'. *I Tatti Studies in the Italian Renaissance*, 19, 1: 93–113. https://doi.org/10.1086/685697

Hilaire-Pérez, Liliane, and Catherine Verna. (2006). 'Dissemination of Technical Knowledge in the Middle Ages and the Early Modern Era: New Approaches and Methodological Issues'. *Technology and Culture*, 47, 3: 536–65.

Hitchcock, David. (2020). 'The Vagrant Poor'. In Hitchcock and McClure, eds., *The Routledge History of Poverty*, 60–78.

Hitchcock, David. (2016). *Vagrancy in English Culture and Society, 1650–1750*. London: Bloomsbury.

Hitchcock, David, and Julia McClure, eds. (2020). *The Routledge History of Poverty, c.1450–1800*. London: Routledge.

Höfele, Andreas, and Werner Von Koppenfels. (2011). 'Introduction'. In Werner Von Koppenfels and Andreas Höfele, eds., *Renaissance Go-Betweens*. Berlin: De Gruyter; first published 2005, 1–14.

Holmberg, Eva Johanna, ed. (2019). *Renaissance and Early Modern Travel – Practice and Experience, 1500–1700*. Special Issue of *Renaissance Studies*, 33, 4.

Horden, Peregrine. (2008). 'Travel Sickness: Medicine and Mobility in the Mediterranean from Antiquity to the Renaissance'. In his *Hospitals and Healing*. Aldershot: Ashgate, 179–99.

Horodowich, Elizabeth. (2018). *The Venetian Discovery of America: Geographic Imagination and Print Culture in the Age of Encounters*. Cambridge: Cambridge University Press.

Hunter, Judith. (2002). 'English Inns, Taverns, Alehouses and Brandy Shops: The Legislative Framework 1495–1797'. In Kümin and Tlusty, *World of the Tavern*, 65–82.

Hyde, Jenni. (2018). *Singing the News: Ballads in Mid-Tudor England*. London: Routledge.

Imhof, Dirk. (2020). 'Plantin, a Publisher Forever on the Road'. In Werner van Hoof, ed., *On the Road with Plantin*. Antwerp: Museum Plantin-Moretus, 26–39.

Inì, Marina. (2021). 'Materiality, Quarantine and Contagion in the Early Modern Mediterranean'. *Social History of Medicine*, 34, 4: 1161–84. https://doi.org/10.1093/shm/hkaa124

Iordannou, Ioanna. (2019). *Venice's Secret Service: Organizing Intelligence in the Renaissance*. Oxford: Oxford University Press.

Jacob, Margaret C. (2006). *Strangers Nowhere in the World: The Rise of Cosmopolitanism in Early Modern Europe*. Philadelphia: University of Pennsylvania Press.

Jaffe-Berg, Erith. (2016). *Commedia dell'arte and the Mediterranean: Charting Journeys and Mapping 'Others'*. London: Routledge.

Judde de Larivière, Claire, and Maartje Van Gelder, eds. (2020). *Popular Politics in an Aristocratic Republic: Political Conflict and Social Contestation in Late Medieval and Early Modern Venice*. Abingdon: Routledge.

Jütte, Daniel. (2014). 'Entering a City: On a Lost Early Modern Practice'. *Urban History*, 41, 2: 204–27. https://doi.org/10.1017/S096392681300062X

Jütte, Robert. (1994). *Poverty and Deviance in Early Modern Europe*. Cambridge: Cambridge University Press.

Kafadar, Cemal. (1986). 'A Death in Venice (1575). Anatolian Muslim Merchants Trading in the Serenissima'. *Journal of Turkish Studies*, 10: 191–217.

Kamp, Jeannette. (2018). 'Controlling Strangers. Identifying Migrants in Early Modern Frankfurt-am-Main'. In Greefs and Winter, *Migration Policies*, 46–65.

Kümin, Beat. (2007). *Drinking Matters. Public Houses and Social Exchange in Early Modern Central Europe*. Houndmills, Basingstoke: Palgrave Macmillan.

Kümin, Beat, and B. Ann Tlusty, eds. (2011). *Public Drinking in the Early Modern World: Voices from the Tavern, 1500–1800*, vols 1 and 3. London: Routledge.

Kümin, Beat, and B. Ann Tlusty, eds. (2002). *The World of the Tavern: Public Houses in Early Modern Europe*. Aldershot: Ashgate.

Lowe, K.J.P. (2015). 'The Global Population of Renaissance Lisbon: Diversity and its Entanglements'. In Gschwend and Lowe, *The Global City*, 57–85.

Lucassen, Jan, and Leo Lucassen. (2009). 'The Mobility Transition Revisited, 1500–1900: What the Case of Europe Can Offer to Global History'. *Journal of Global History*, 4, 3: 347–77. https://doi.org/10.1017/S174002280999012X

Luu, Lien Bich. (2005). *Immigrants and the Industries of London, 1500–1700*. Aldershot: Ashgate.

Maczak, Antoni. (1995). *Travel in Early Modern Europe*, trans. by Ursula Phillips. Cambridge: Polity Press; original Polish edition 1980.

Malagnini, Francesca. (2017). *Il Lazzaretto Nuovo di Venezia. Le scritture parietali*. Florence: Franco Cesati Editore.

Mansell, Charmian. (2021). 'Beyond the Home: Space and Agency in the Experiences of Female Service in Early Modern England'. *Gender & History*, 33, 1: 24–49. https://doi.org/10.1111/1468-0424.12494

Martin, Meredith, and Daniela Bleichmar. (2015). 'Introduction: Objects in Motion in the Early Modern World'. *Art History*, 38, 4: 604–19.

Martinez, Miguel. (2016). *Front Lines: Soldiers' Writing in the Early Modern Hispanic World*. Philadephia: University of Pennsylvania Press.

Massai, Sonia. (2005). 'John Wolfe and the Impact of Exemplary Go-Betweens on Early Modern Print Culture'. In Von Koppenfels and Höfele, *Renaissance Go-Betweens*, 104–18. https://doi.org/10.1515/9783110919516.104

Matt, Susan J. (2011). *Homesickness: An American History*. Oxford: Oxford University Press.

Maudlin, Daniel. (2020). 'Inns and Elite Mobility in Late Georgian Britain'. *Past & Present*, 247, 1: 37–76. https://doi.org/10.1093/pastj/gtz050

Mazzei, Rita. (2013). *Per terra e per acqua. Viaggi e viaggiatori nell'Europa moderna.* Rome: Carocci.

McKee, Sally. (2008). 'Domestic Slavery in Renaissance Italy'. *Slavery & Abolition*, 29, 3: 305–26. https://doi.org/10.1080/01440390802267774

McIlvenna, Una. (2016). 'When the News was Sung'. *Media History*, 22, 3–4: 317–33. http://doi.10.1080/13688804.2016.1211930

McShane, Angela. (2019). 'Political Street Songs and Singers in Seventeenth-Century England'. In Degl'Innocenti and Rospocher, *Street Singers*, 94–118. https://doi.org/10.1111/rest.12534

Meer, Marcus. (2021). 'Seeing Proof of Townsmen on the Move: Coats of Arms, Chivalric Badges, and Travel in the Later Middle Ages'. In Gonzalez Martin, Salzberg, and Zenobi, *Cities in Motion*, 11–38. https://doi.org/10.1163/15700658-BJA10034

Meeus, Bruno, Bas Van Heur, and Karel Arnaut. (2019). 'Migration and the Infrastructural Politics of Urban Arrival'. In Bruno Meeus, Bas Van Heur, and Karel Arnaut, eds., *Arrival Infrastructures: Migration and Urban Social Mobilities*. London: Palgrave Macmillan, 1–32. http://doi:10.1007/978-3-319-91167-0_1

Metcalf, Alida C. (2005). *Go-Betweens and the Colonization of Brazil 1500–1600*. Austin: University of Texas Press.

Midura, Rachel. (2020). 'Masters of the Post. Northern Italy and European Communications Networks, 1530–1730'. PhD thesis, Stanford University, California.

Midura, Rachel. (2019). 'Publishing the Baroque Post: The Postal Itinerary and the Mailbag Novel'. In Findlen and Sutherland, *The Renaissance of Letters*, 255–71.

Minuzzi, Sabrina. (2020). *La peste e la stampa: Venezia nel XVI e XVII secolo*. Venice: Marsilio.

Moatti, Claudia, ed. (2004). *La mobilité des personnes en Méditerranée de l'antiquité a l'époque moderne: procédures de contrôle et documents d'identification*. Rome: École Francaise de Rome.

Modigliani, Anna. (1999). 'Taverne e osterie a Roma nel tardo medioevo: tipologia, uso degli spazi, arredo e distribuzione nella città'. In *Taverne, locande e stufe a Roma nel Rinascimento*. Rome: Roma nel Rinascimento, 19–45.

Molà, Luca. (2010). 'La Repubblica di Venezia tra acque dolci e acque salse: investimenti tecnologici a Lizzafusina nel Rinascimento'. In Arturo Calzona and Daniela Lamberini, eds., *La civiltà delle acque tra Medioevo e Rinascimento, Atti del convegno (Mantova 1–4 ottobre 2008)*. Florence: Olschki, 447–72.

Motta, Emilio. (1898). 'Albergatori milanesi nei secoli XIV e XV'. *Archivio storico lombardo*, 25, 366–77.

Nelles, Paul, and Rosa Salzberg, eds. (2023). *Connected Mobilities in the Early Modern World: The Practice and Experience of Movement*. Amsterdam: Amsterdam University Press.

Nevola, Fabrizio. (2021). *Street Life in Renaissance Italy*. New Haven, CT: Yale University Press.

Nordman, Daniel. (1987). 'Sauf-conduits et passeports, en France, à la Renaissance'. In Jean Ceard and Jean-Claude Margolin, eds. *Voyager à la Renaissance*. Paris: Maisonneuve et Larose, 145–58.

Page Moch, Leslie. (1992). *Moving Europeans: Migration in Western Europe since 1650*, Bloomington: Indiana University Press.

Palmer, Barbara D. (2005). 'Early Modern Mobility: Players, Payments, and Patrons'. *Shakespeare Quarterly*, 56, 3: 259–305. https://doi.org/10.1353/shq.2006.0010

Palumbo-Fossati, Isabella. (2006). 'Venise, porte du Levant: aspects linguistiques et echos d'orient a travers les objets presents dans la maison venitienne au xvi'. In Michel Bozdemir and Sonel Bosnali, eds. *Contact des langues II: Les mots voyageurs et l'Orient*. Istanbul: University of Bogaziçi.

Parker, Charles H. (2010). *Global Interactions in the Early Modern Age, 1400–1800*. Cambridge: Cambridge University Press.

Pedani, Maria Pia. (1994). *In nome del gran signore: inviati ottomani a Venezia dalla caduta di Costantinopoli alla guerra di Candia*. Venice: Deputazione Ditrice.

Pedani, Maria Pia, and Paola Issa. (2016). 'Il viaggio dell'arabo Ra'd di Aleppo a Venezia (1654–1656)'. *Mediterranea – ricerche storiche*, 375–400.

Petrella, Giancarlo. (2013). 'Ippolito Ferrarese, a Traveling "Cerretano" and Publisher in Sixteenth-Century Italy'. In Benito Rial Costas, ed. *Print Culture and Peripheries in Early Modern Europe*. Leiden: Brill, 201–26.

Pettegree, Andrew. (2014). *The Invention of News: How the World Came to Know About Itself*. New Haven, CT: Yale University Press.

Peyer, Hans Conrad. (2009). *Viaggiare nel medioevo. Dall'ospitalità alla locanda*, trans. by Nicola Antonacci. Rome: Laterza; first published in German 1987.

Pooley, Colin G. (2017). 'Connecting Historical Studies of Transport, Mobility and Migration'. *Journal of Transport History*, 38, 2: 251–9. https://doi.org/10.1177/0022526617715538

Pratt, Mary Louise. (1992). *Imperial Eyes: Travel Writing and Transculturation*. London: Routledge.

Preiser-Kapeller, Johannes, Lucian Reinfandt, and Yannis Stouraitis, eds. (2020). *Migration Histories of the Medieval Afroeurasian Transition Zone: Aspects of Mobility between Africa, Asia and Europe, 300–1500 C.E.* Leiden: Brill. https://doi.org/10.1163/9789004425613

Quillien, Robin, and Solène Rivoal. (2020). 'Boatmen, Fishermen, and Venetian Institutions: From Negotiation to Confrontation'. In Judde de Larivière and Van Gelder, *Popular Politics*, 197–216.

Quirk, Joel, and Darshan Vigneswaran. (2015). 'Mobility Makes States'. In Joel Quirk and Darshan Vigneswaran, eds., *Mobility Makes States: Migration and Power in Africa*. Philadelphia: Pennsylvania University Press, 1–34.

Raj, Kapil. (2016). 'Go-Betweens, Travelers, and Cultural Translators'. In Bernard Lightman, ed., *A Companion to the History of Science*. Chichester Malden: John Wiley & Sons, 39–57.

Reeves, Nathan. (2021). 'Music, Mobility, and Galley Servitude in Spanish Naples'. Paper delivered at the Renaissance Society of America Annual Meeting (online).

Riello, Giorgio. (2010). 'The Material Culture of Walking: Spaces of Methodologies in the Long Eighteenth Century'. In Tara Hamling and Catherine Richardson, eds., *Everyday Objects: Medieval and Early Modern Material Culture and Its Meanings*. Farnham, Surrey: Ashgate, 41–56.

Rizzi, Andrea. (2021). 'Interpreting in Early Modern Diplomacy: Occasional Mobility and the Liminal Spaces of Trust'. *Renaissance and Reformation/ Renaissance et Réforme*, 44, 1: 49–68.

Roche, Daniel, ed. (2000). *La ville promise. Mobilités et accueil à Paris fin xviie-début xixe siècle*. Paris: Fayard.

Roche, Daniel. (2003). *Humeurs vagabondes. De la circulation des hommes et de l'utilité des voyages*. Paris: Fayard.

Rollison, David. (1999). 'Exploding England: The Dialectics of Mobility and Settlement in Early Modern England'. *Social History*, 24, 1: 1–16.

Romani, Mario. (1948). *Pellegrini e viaggiatori nell'economia di Roma dal xiv al xvii secolo*. Milan: Società editrice 'Vita e pensiero'.

Ronchi, Oliviero. (1967). 'Alloggi di scolari a Padova nei secoli XIII–XVIII'. *Bollettino del Museo Civico di Padova*, 56: 293–319.

Rothman, E. Natalie. (2021). *The Dragoman Renaissance: Diplomatic Interpreters and the Routes of Orientalism*. Ithaca, NY: Cornell University Press.

Rothman, E. Natalie. (2011). *Brokering Empire: Trans-Imperial Subjects Between Venice and Istanbul*. Ithaca, NY: Cornell University Press.

Rubiés, Joan-Pau. (2017). 'Ethnography and Cultural Translation in the Early Modern Missions'. *Studies in Church History*, 53: 272–310. http://doi:10.1017/stc.2016.17

Ruggiero, Guido. (2015). *The Renaissance in Italy: A Social and Cultural History of the Rinascimento*. Cambridge: Cambridge University Press.

Saletti, Beatrice. (2017). 'Entering the City. The Arrival of Foreigners in Late Medieval Bologna'. Paper delivered at the conference *Mobility and Space in Late Medieval and Early Modern Europe*, Oxford University.

Salzberg, Rosa. (2021). 'Little Worlds in Motion: Mobility and Space in the *osterie* of Early Modern Venice'. *Journal of Early Modern History*, 25, 1–2, 96–117. http://doi.10.1163/15700658-BJA10033

Salzberg, Rosa. (2020). 'Peddling and the Informal Economy'. In Hitchcock and McClure, *The Routledge History of Poverty*, 293–308.

Salzberg, Rosa. (2019). 'Mobility, Cohabitation and Cultural Exchange in the Lodging Houses of Early Modern Venice'. *Urban History*, 46, 3: 398–418. http://doi.10.1017/S0963926818000536

Salzberg, Rosa. (2018). 'Controlling and Documenting Migration via Urban "Spaces of Arrival" in Early Modern Venice'. In Greefs and Winter, *Migration Policies*, 27–45.

Salzberg, Rosa. (2017). 'The Margins in the Centre: Working Around Rialto (Venice, 16th Century)'. In Andrew Spicer and Jane Stevens Crawshaw, eds., *The Place of the Social Margins, 1400–1800*. London: Routledge, 135–52.

Salzberg, Rosa. (2016). '"Poverty Makes Me Invisible": Street Singers and Hard Times in Italian Renaissance Cities'. *Italian Studies*, 71, 2: 212–24. http://doi.10.1080/00751634.2016.1175719

Salzberg, Rosa. (2010). 'In the Mouths of Charlatans. Street Performers and the Dissemination of Pamphlets in Renaissance Italy'. *Renaissance Studies*, 24, 5: 638–53. http://doi.10.1111/j.1477–4658.2010.00670.x

Salzberg, Rosa, and Massimo Rospocher. (2012). 'Street Singers in Italian Renaissance Urban Culture and Communication'. *Cultural and Social History*, 9, 1: 9–26. http://doi.10.2752/147800412X13191165982872

Santoro, Marco, and Samanta Segatori, eds. (2013). *Mobilità dei mestieri del libro tra quattrocento e seicento: convegno internazionale, Roma, 14–16 marzo 2012*. Pisa: Fabrizio Serra.

Santus, Cesare. (2019). 'L'accoglienza e il controllo dei pellegrini orientali a Roma. L'ospizio armeno di Santa Maria Egiziaca (XVI-XVIII sec.)'. *Mélanges de l'École française de Rome, Moyen Âge*, 131–2: 447–59.

Sardelic, Mirko. (2022). 'The Late Sixteenth-Century Ship in the Adriatic as a Cultural System'. In Alina Payne, ed., *The Land Between Two Seas: Art on the Move in the Mediterranean and the Black Sea 1300–1700*. Leiden: Brill, 29–39. https://doi.org/10.1163/9789004515468_003

Schobesberger, Nikolaus, et al. (2016). 'European Postal Networks'. In Joad Raymond and Noah Moxham, eds., *News Networks in Early Modern Europe*. Leiden: Brill, 19–63.

Schmitz, Carolin. (2023). 'Travelling for Health: Local and Regional Mobility of Patients in Early Modern Rural Spain'. In Nelles and Salzberg, *Connected Mobilities*, 88–110.

Scholz, Luca. (2020). *Borders and Freedom of Movement in the Holy Roman Empire*. Oxford: Oxford University Press.

Scott, Hamish. (2015). 'Travel and Communications'. In Hamish Scott, ed., *The Oxford Handbook of Early Modern History: 1350–1750 – Volume I: People and Place*. Oxford: Oxford University Press, 166–92.

Semi, Francesca. (1983). *Gli ospizi di Venezia*. Venice: Istituzioni di recovero e educazione.

Sennefelt, Karin. (2018). 'Ordering Identification: Migrants, Material Culture and Social Bonds in Stockholm, 1650–1720'. In Greefs and Winter, *Migration Policies*, 66–86.

Siebenhühner, Kim. 2008. 'Conversion, Mobility, and the Roman Inquisition in Italy around 1600'. Past and Present, 200, 1: 5–35. https://doi.org/10.1093/pastj/gtn012

Simeoni, Luigi. (1934). 'L'ufficio dei forestieri a Bologna dal sec. xiv al xvi'. *Atti e memorie della R. deputazione di storia patria per le provincie di Romagna*, 24, 3: 71–95.

Spoturno, María Laura. (2014). 'Revisiting Malinche: A Study of Her Role as an Interpreter'. In Federici and Tessicini, *Translators, Interpreters*, 121–35. https://doi.org/10.1057/9781137400048_8

Spufford, Margaret. (1984). *The Great Reclothing of Rural England: Petty Chapmen and their Wares in the Seventeenth Century*. London: Hambledon Press.

Stagl, Justin. (2002). *A History of Curiosity: The Theory of Travel 1550–1800*. London: Routledge.

Stevens Crawshaw, Jane. (2015). 'The Renaissance Invention of Quarantine'. In Linda Clark and Carol Rawcliffe, eds., *The Fifteenth Century XII: Society in an Age of Plague*. Woodbridge: Boydell & Brewer, 161–74.

Subrahmanyan, Sanjay. (2011). *Three Ways to Be Alien: Travails and Encounters in the Early Modern World*. Waltham, MA: Brandeis University Press.

Susini, Fabiana. (2018). 'From the Grand Tour to the Grand Hotel: The Birth of the Hospitality Industry in the Grand Duchy of Tuscany between the 17th and 19th Centuries'. *Architectural Histories*, 6, 1: 1–10.

Sweet, Rosemary. (2012). *Cities and the Grand Tour: The British in Italy, c.1690–1820*. Cambridge: Cambridge University Press. https://doi.org/10.1017/CBO9781139104197

Terpstra, Nicholas. (2015). *Religious Refugees in the Early Modern World: An Alternative History of the Reformation*. Cambridge: Cambridge University Press.

Tessicini, Dario. (2014). 'Introduction: Translators, Interpreters, and Cultural Negotiation'. In Federici and Tessicini, *Translators, Interpreters*, 1–9. http://doi.10.1057/9781137400048_1

Tlusty, B. Ann. (2001). *Bacchus and Civic Order: The Culture of Drink in Early Modern Germany*. Charlottesville: University of Virginia Press.

Toffolo, Sandra. (2022). 'The Pilgrim, the City and the Book: The Role of the Mobility of Pilgrims in Book Circulation in Renaissance Venice'. In Arthur der Weduwen and Malcolm Walsby, eds., *The Book World of Early Modern Europe: Essays in Honour of Andrew Pettegree, Volume 2*. Leiden: Brill, 131–53. https://doi.org/10.1163/9789004518100_010

Toffolo, Sandra. (2018). 'Pellegrini stranieri e il commercio veneziano nel Rinascimento'. In Elisa Gregori, ed., *Rinascimento fra il Veneto e l'Europa: Questioni, metodi, percorsi*. Padua: Cleup, 263–84.

Trivellato, Francesca. (2010). 'Review Article: Renaissance Italy and the Muslim Mediterranean in Recent Historical Work'. *Journal of Modern History*, 82, 1: 127–55.

Trivellato, Francesca. (2007). 'Merchants' Letters Across Geographical and Social Boundaries'. In Francisco Bethencourt and Florike Egmond, eds. *Correspondence and Cultural Exchange in Europe, 1400–1700*. Cambridge: Cambridge University Press, 80–103.

Tuliani, Maurizio. (1994). *Osti, avventori e malandrini. Luoghi di sosta e di ritrovo nella Siena del Trecento*. Siena: Protagon Editori Toscani.

Urry, John. (2007). *Mobilities*. Cambridge: Cambridge University Press.

Van den Heuvel, Danielle. (2015). 'Policing Pedlars. The Prosecution of Illegal Street Trade in Eighteenth-century Dutch Towns'. *Historical Journal*, 58, 2: 367–92.

Van den Heuvel, Danielle. (2012). 'Selling in the Shadows: Peddlers and Hawkers in Early Modern Europe'. In Marcel van der Linden and Leo Lucassen, eds., *Working on Labor: Essays in Honor of Jan Lucassen*. Leiden: Brill, 125–51. https://doi.org/10.1163/9789004231443_007

Van Gelder, Maartje, and Tijana Krstić. (2015). 'Introduction: Cross-Confessional Diplomacy and Diplomatic Intermediaries in the Early Modern Mediterranean'. *Journal of Early Modern History*, *19*, 2–3: 93–105. https://doi.org/10.1163/15700658-12342452

Verdon, Jean. (2003). *Travel in the Middle Ages*, trans. by George Holoch. Notre Dame, IN: University of Notre Dame Press; first published in French, 1998.

Verhoeven, Gerrit. (2023). 'Wading Through the Mire. Mobility on the Grand Tour (1585–1750)'. In Nelles and Salzberg, *Connected Mobilities*, 63–85.

Verhoeven, Gerrit. (2019). 'Not for Weaker Vessels?! Travel and Gender in the Early Modern Low Countries'. In Floris Meens and Tim Sintobin, eds., *Gender, Companionship, and Travel: Discourses in Pre-Modern and Modern Travel Literature*. London: Routledge, 66–78.

Walden, Justine A. (2020). 'Muslim Slaves in Early Modern Rome. The Development and Visibility of a Labouring Class'. In Matthew Coneys Wainwright and Emily Michelson, eds., *A Companion to Religious Minorities in Early Modern Rome*. Leiden: Brill, 298–323. https://doi.org/10.1163/9789004443495_012

Wilson, Bronwen. (2005). *The World in Venice: Print, the City, and Early Modern Identity*. Toronto: University of Toronto Press.

Young Kim, David. (2014). *The Traveling Artist in the Italian Renaissance: Geography, Mobility, and Style*. New Haven, CT: Yale University Press.

Zaniboni, Eugenio. (1921). *Alberghi italiani e viaggiatori stranieri sec. xiii-xvii*. Naples: Detken & Rocholl.

Zemon Davis, Natalie. (2006). *Trickster Travels: A Sixteenth-Century Muslim Between Worlds*. New York: Farrar, Straus and Giroux/Hill and Wang.

Zenobi, Luca. (2018). *Borders and the Politics of Space in Late Medieval Italy: Milan, Venice and their Territories in the Fifteenth Century*. PhD thesis, University of Oxford.

Zur Nieden, Gesa, and Berthold Over, eds. (2016). *Musicians' Mobilities and Music Migrations in Early Modern Europe: Biographical Patterns and Cultural Exchanges*. Bielefeld: transcript-Verlag, 2016.

Acknowledgements

I would particularly like to thank Beat Kümin, Paul Nelles, and Sandra Toffolo for their comments on earlier drafts of this work, as well as the editors, John Henderson, Jonathan Nelson, and Sarah McBryde, and the anonymous readers for their input and suggestions. The ideas for this Element were able to percolate thanks to a generous grant from the European Union's Horizon 2020 research and innovation programme (Marie Skłodowska-Curie grant agreement No 702296) which also allowed me to organize a conference on the theme of Renaissance mobility at the European University Institute in 2018. I am grateful to the participants in that conference for sharing their inspiring work and the conversations that have continued since then. Finally, I dedicate this Element to my family who have, as ever, provided support, love, and delightful distraction over the time it was written.

Cambridge Elements

The Renaissance

John Henderson

Birkbeck, University of London, and Wolfson College, University of Cambridge

John Henderson is Professor of Italian Renaissance History at Birkbeck, University of London, and Emeritus Fellow of Wolfson College, University of Cambridge. His recent publications include *Florence Under Siege: Surviving Plague in an Early Modern City* (2019), and *Plague and the City*, edited with Lukas Engelmann and Christos Lynteris (2019), and *Representing Infirmity: Diseased Bodies in Renaissance Italy*, edited with Fredrika Jacobs and Jonathan K. Nelson (2021). He is also the author of *Piety and Charity in Late Medieval Florence* (1994); *The Great Pox: The French Disease in Renaissance Europe*, with Jon Arrizabalaga and Roger French (1997); and *The Renaissance Hospital: Healing the Body and Healing the Soul* (2006).

Jonathan K. Nelson

Syracuse University Florence, and Kennedy School, Harvard University

Jonathan K. Nelson teaches Italian Renaissance Art at Syracuse University Florence and is research associate at the Harvard Kennedy School. His books include *Filippino Lippi* (2004, with Patrizia Zambrano); *Leonardo e la reinvenzione della figura femminile* (2007), *The Patron's Payoff: Conspicuous Commissions in Italian Renaissance Art* (2008, with Richard J. Zeckhauser); and he co-edited *Representing Infirmity. Diseased Bodies in Renaissance Italy* (2021). He co-curated museum exhibitions dedicated to Michelangelo (2002), Botticelli and Filippino (2004), Robert Mapplethorpe (2009), and Marcello Guasti (2019), and two online exhibitions about Bernard Berenson (2012, 2015). Forthcoming publications include a monograph on Filippino (Reaktion Books, 2022) and an Element, *The Risky Business of Renaissance Art*.

Assistant Editor

Sarah McBryde, *Birkbeck, University of London*

Editorial Board

Wendy Heller, Scheide Professor of Music History, *Princeton University*
Giorgio Riello, Chair of Early Modern Global History, *European University Institute, Florence*
Ulinka Rublack, Professor of Early Modern History, St Johns College, *University of Cambridge*
Jane Tylus, Andrew Downey Orrick Professor of Italian and Professor of Comparative Literature, *Yale University*

About the series

Timely, concise, and authoritative, Elements in the Renaissance showcases cutting-edge scholarship by both new and established academics. Designed to introduce students, researchers, and general readers to key questions in current research, the volumes take multi-disciplinary and transnational approaches to explore the conceptual, material, and cultural frameworks that structured Renaissance experience.

Printed in the United States
by Baker & Taylor Publisher Services